THE
LITTLE
BOOK
OF
LEICESTERSHIRE

NATASHA SHELDON

To my nans,
Doris, Irene and Lillian,
who helped ignite my love of history.

First published 2017

The History Press
The Mill, Brimscombe Port
Stroud, Gloucestershire, GL5 2QG
www.thehistorypress.co.uk

British Library Cataloguing in Publication Data.
A catalogue record for this book is available from the British Library.

ISBN 978 0 7509 6734 1

Typesetting and origination by The History Press
Printed and bound in Great Britain by TJ International Ltd

CONTENTS

ABOUT THE AUTHOR

NATASHA SHELDON lives in Leicester and studied Ancient History and Archaeology at the city's university. Passionate about local history, archaeology and travel writing, she is the author of *Not a Guide to Leicester* and *Leicester in 100 Dates* with The History Press, and is also the columnist for the online site Decoded Past (www.decodedpast.com).

INTRODUCTION

The name *Laegrecastrescir* was first recoded in 1087. But Leicestershire is much older.

To the Saxons it was the Kingdom of Mercia. To the Romans it was at the hub of Roman Britain. To the Celts it was the land of the Corieltauvi, a fierce warlike tribe. To the Vikings it was part of the Dane law.

Leicestershire has so often been the backdrop for many of the turning points in British history. Kings have been killed and buried here, and royal dynasties have changed. Leicestershire has been the birthplace of rebels and heroes, movers and shakers, who have changed Britain and even the world.

Leicestershire's land has its own unique character, shaped long ago. Its geology has dictated the industries that have made Leicestershire's towns great and the foods that have made the county famous.

Leicestershire has always been a meeting place of people and a melting pot of cultures from prehistory, and no more so than today. It is one of Britain's most diverse counties and its most recent incomers have only enriched the county's already rich scheme of traditions

To include everything about Leicestershire in a book of this size is impossible. Instead, I have tried to concentrate on producing a potted history, using whimsical, amusing, little known and occasionally disturbing tales, facts and anecdotes that illustrate everything that makes Leicestershire unique.

It is my hope that this brief journey through Leicestershire's past and present will amuse and inform in equal measure.

Natasha Sheldon
2017

NATURAL LEICESTER

THE MAKING OF LEICESTERSHIRE

Leicestershire marks the centre of England – or rather, the geographical centre of England is in Leicestershire. This landmark spot is at Ordinance Survey ref. SP 36373.66, 96143.05, which falls at Lindley Hall Farm, near Fenny Drayton and Higham.

The county shares its borders with Rutland, Northamptonshire, Warwickshire, Derbyshire, Lincolnshire and Staffordshire. Within those borders are 208,289 hectares of farmland, woodland and towns.

But this wasn't always the case …

The Story of the Land
In the beginning there was lava – lots of lava.

Some 600 million years ago, Precambrian Leicestershire was submerged under a shallow sea, studded with volcanic islands. The islands constantly spewed out ash and lava, which eventually formed the county's oldest layers of igneous rock. These rocks, visible in the Charnwood region around Blackbrook Reservoir and Switherland Wood, are one of England's few exposures of Precambrian rock.

Bardon Hill, an extinct volcano in north-west Leicestershire, is a relic of those times. It is also the highest point in Leicestershire, reaching 912ft above sea level. John Curtis, a nineteenth-century entomologist, described it as 'one of the most extraordinary points of view in nature'. Even today, the view from the hill's summit in clear weather allows views of Shropshire, the Malvern Hills and the not so distant Lincoln Cathedral.

Time passed. The primal sea retreated and the mud it left behind began to form into Leicestershire's famous Switherland Slate. Not long afterwards, the magmas began to cool to form the pink and grey granite of Mountsorrel, which today is the location of the largest quarry in Europe.

About 420 million years ago, Leicestershire and the rest of the landmass it occupied, was on the move. This seismic relocation wrinkled the land. In Leicestershire, one of these folds survives as the Thringston Fault, which forms the eastern border between Leicestershire and Derbyshire.

The fault line also acted as a border for the Leicestershire coalfield in the north of the county. These coalfields were formed in the carboniferous era, when the warm primal seas that had re-flooded the land drained to become swamps and forests which in their turn died away to become coal. At the same time limestone deposits were forming around the area of Grace Dieu.

At the end of this era the rivers took over, depositing fluvial deposits to form Shepshed Sandstone.

Further west, much of Leicestershire's landscape is mainly deposits of boulder and Liassic clay, dropped by busy glaciers during the last ice age. The ice formed many of Leicestershire's valleys such as the Vale of Belvoir. Just north of the vale is the lowest point in Leicestershire where the land dips to just 24.8m above sea level. It can be found just along a bend in a minor road near Bottesford and the River Devon, near the border with Northamptonshire.

FOSSILS AND DINOSAURS

The Leicester Mammoth

On 28 October 1863, a strange object was found during the construction of a sewer off Belgrave Road. The object was 9ft 7in long and 2ft in circumference. It would have been longer but, unfortunately, the workmen who discovered it unwittingly 'lost' 2-3ft of it before they realised they had something unusual on their hands.

Once discovered, the workmen were unsure quite what it was they had found – only that it wasn't modern. After some debate, they settled on it being an old Roman column, but called in the experts to be on the safe side.

The 'column' was sent to local geologist, Mr James Plant, who declared it to be the tusk of *elephas primigenius* – a mammoth.

An excited Mr Plant hotfooted it to the site and was fortunate to find the ground undisturbed. The tusk had been discovered on a 3ft layer of red marl dating to around 180 million years ago. However, Plant concluded that the beast was not contemporary with this layer. Instead, its body had sunk through younger, softer gravel above until it came to rest on the more ancient layers. This dated the mammoth to 20,000 years ago.

The Leicester mammoth made the national headlines, with even *The Times* taking an interest in the doings of the Leicester drain. Experts arrived and declared that at 16ft, the tusk was even larger that the specimen in the British Museum.

The Barrow Kipper

Barrow upon Soar is famous for a plesiosaur of the species *Rhomaleosaurus megacephalus* – nicknamed the 'Barrow Kipper' – excavated there in 1851. The dinosaur was found in a lime pit outside the village.

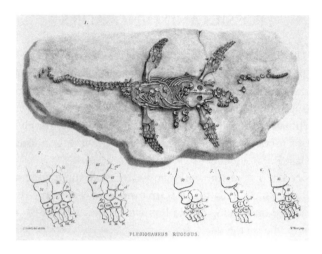

PLESIOSAURUS RUGOSUS.

The skeleton is on display at the New Walk Museum in Leicester, with a full-size replica at Charnwood Museum in Loughborough. But Barrow marks the Kipper in its own way, with a sign on the roundabout in the centre of the village commemorating its oldest resident.

Charnia masoni

Charnwood Forest was the site of the first ever-recorded discovery of *Charnia masoni*, the earliest known large, complex fossilised species on record.

The fossil was named after the place it was found and its finder, local schoolboy Roger Mason. In 1957, Roger and some friends were exploring a quarry near the Charnwood village of Woodhouse Eaves when he discovered imprints in a rock like the fronds of a fern.

The imprint turned out to be neither plant nor animal but a kind of pre-animal, the first evidence that complex multicellular life existed in the Precambrian era. Charnwood is the only place in Western Europe where these Precambrian fossils have been found.

RIVERS AND WATERWAYS

The River Soar is Leicestershire's principle river, bisecting the county from north to south. The Soar's name comes from *ser*, to flow, which it shares with other European rivers such as the Seine.

The source of the Soar in Leicestershire is between Hinckley and Lutterworth. From there, the river runs down through the county to Leicester, along the fertile Soar Valley until it joins the River Trent at the county boundary at Trent Lock.

After the Industrial Revolution, the Soar turned a most unnatural shade of pink due to discharges from the textile industry. However, a clean up by the Environment Agency has returned the river to a less disturbing and more natural shade.

Industrial discharges are now carefully monitored. But it is more usual in the twenty-first century to find deposits of ashes rather than emissions in the Soar.

In 2004, the *Telegraph* reported how 250,000 requests to the Environment Agency from Leicestershire Sikhs and Hindus led to permission being granted for the Soar to stand in for the River Ganges at funerals. The reason for this request was to avoid the prohibitive costs of travelling to India to use the original sacred river.

The Soar has a number of tributaries, namely Soar Brook, Thurlaston Brook, the River Biam, Rothley Brook, Black Brook, Whetstone Brook, the River Sense, the River Wreake and Kingston Brook.

The Rivers Wreake and Eye
This major tributary of the River Soar is in fact two rivers in one. For the 6 miles before it reaches Melton Mowbray, the river is known as the Eye, but, once past the town, it changes its name and character to become the Wreake.

The clue to this duel naming is in the meaning of the words. The initial stretch of the waterway is calm and unremarkable, hence 'Eye' which comes from the old English *ēa* for 'the river'.

But the Norse invaders of the eighth century were clearly more impressed with the latter stretch, which gave them great trouble and led them to rename this part as the Wreake, after their word for twisting and meandering.

Rothley Brook

Rothley Brook forms a southern boundary around Charnwood Forest, beginning at Bagworth and ending when it joins the River Soar at Rothley, the place after which it is named today, although once it was known as 'Heather Brook' or 'Great Brook'.

The brook is a haven for wild bird life, with over forty species of birds identified including kingfishers, great spotted woodpeckers and little and tawny owls.

The River Sence

The Sence has its origins at Copt Oak in Leicestershire before leaving the county and joining the River Anker on the Warwickshire border. In the nineteenth century, there were at least eight watermills along the river.

The River Smite

The Smite originates from a number of springs near Holwell, one of Leicestershire's many chalybeate springs. In the seventeenth and eighteenth centuries the water from the spring was considered to have healing properties, and was laid out with stone seating for those that took the waters. The spring contains iron salts, which gives it a reddish colour, and it is considered to have a distinctive sulphur taste.

The River Mease

The River Mease and the lower part of one of its tributaries, the Gilwiskaw (pronounced *jill-a-whiskey*) Brook, are both protected as 'one of the best examples of an unspoilt meandering lowland river'.

Groby Pool

Lying on the edge of Charnwood Forest, Groby Pool is the largest expanse of water in the county. It may not all be natural however, owing its formation to Roman clay extraction, and damning of the slate brook by medieval monks from Leicester Abbey.

Floods

Flooding is not a modern phenomenon in Leicestershire. The unruly waters of its rivers, which can run amok during heavy rainfall, have long provoked the county.

In May 1932, the village of Croft was drenched with rain for three to four days. The waterlogged ground could finally hold no more water and inhabitants were stranded in the upper storeys of their homes, with rescuers having to reach them by boat.

In Wymeswold, the River Mantle would also regularly break its banks. The flooding was so bad that boys would launch a boat down the aptly named Brook Street, which was in fact the village's main road.

In 1881, the Improvement Bill meant Leicester's corporation could build flood defences to protect the town and its outlying areas from the floods that periodically plagued it.

Unfortunately, the defences were not completed in time to deal with the heavy rainfall of March 1889. The rain had been falling for days but on 8 March it intensified with 1¾in falling in twenty-four hours. The land was waterlogged and timber sleepers used in the half-finished flood defences were washed downstream by the water, causing a blockage that resulted in the very flooding they were meant to prevent.

By 3 p.m. that afternoon, low lying areas such as Oxford Street and Aylestone Road were under water, with factory cellars so severely flooded that premises had to close. By 6 p.m., town residents were taking refuge in upstairs rooms as 'the streets themselves assumed the character of canals.'

Other Leicester Rivers
   The River Avon
   The River Chater
   Derwent Mouth
   The River Jordan
   The River Swift
   The River Whipling
   The River Tweed

FORESTS AND WOODS

Only 4 per cent of Leicestershire is wooded, with 2 per cent of that composed of ancient woodland. Leicestershire has a total of 100 woods in this category – and that's not including the national forests and other woodland still in progress.

Charnwood Forest
Seven miles north-west of Leicester, Charnwood Forest occupies the oldest rocky and wild tracts of land in the county. Its name derives from *cerne woda*, from the Celtic *carn*, meaning cairn, and the Old English *wudu*, meaning wood.

   The forest is an important recreational area, with woodland walks, noted for their displays of bluebells in the early spring, rock climbing and hillwalking. Popular places with public access include Bardon Hill, Beacon Hill, Bradgate Park, Swithland Wood and the Outwoods, and Stoneywell Cottage.

The National Forest
In 1990, Charnwood Forest acquired a new neighbour. The new National Forest is part of a Countryside Commission incentive to increase woodland in low-forested areas.

   The forest, which also spans Derbyshire and Staffordshire, covers Leicestershire in the old industrial areas of Coalville, Swadlingcote and Ashby de la Zouch. By 2013, the National

Forest had spread sufficiently to increase forestation in these areas affected to 16.5 per cent – and it still continues to grow.

Jubilee Woods

As the name suggests, this 10 hectares of mixed woodland surrounding Beacon Hill County Park was presented to the city council in 1977 to commemorate the Queen's Silver Jubilee.

The woodland was expanded in 2012 to coincide with the Diamond Jubilee. Sixty new woods are to be added, one for every year of Queen Elizabeth II's reign.

Other Leicestershire Woods

    Eyebrook Valley Wood
    Hanging Stone and Outwoods
    Martinshaw Wood
    Bagworth Heath Wood
    Sarah's Wood
    Sheet Hedges Wood
    Coleorton Wood
    Sence Valley Forest
    Great Merrible Wood
    Tugby Wood
    Cloud Wood
    Allexton Wood
    Buddan Wood
    Burbage and Sheepy Woods
    Grace Dieu Wood
    Martinshaw Wood
    Ouston Wood
    Asplin Wood
    Leightfield Wood

PARKS, NATURE RESERVES AND SITES OF SCIENTIFIC INTEREST

Leicestershire has ninety-one Sites of Special Scientific Interest and several nature reserves. Here's just a selection.

Aylestone Meadows

The city of Leicester's largest nature reserve is situated on the floodplains of the rivers Soar and Biam. In 2012, more than 600 species of plants and animals were found on the site including a previously unknown species of willow tree. The tree, which is a hybrid of goat, grey, purple and osier willows, is unique in the world.

According to nature experts, these finds make Aylestone Meadows a 'most extensive area of wildlife'. But these rare species and the meadows themselves could have been lost. In 2011, Leicester City Council planned to build a floodlit football pitch over them – until the resulting outpouring of local feeling changed their minds.

Tilton Railway Cutting and Other Interesting Sites

This disused railway cutting is a window into Leicestershire's geological past. Tilton's rock cliffs, although overgrown, reveal some of the oldest exposed rocks in Leicestershire with ironstone and limestone sediments dating back 189–186 million years ago. The site is also a rich source of fossils, especially brachiopods, which has led to it being declared a Site of Special Scientific Interest.

But the rocks of Charnwood Lodge are older still. Covering 80 hectares of land, the site has rock formations dating back 600 million years – amongst the oldest in England.

The rocks date from Leicestershire's volcanic era when they jostled each other in the pyroclastic flow of the county's Pre-cambrian volcanoes. Age aside, it is rare to find rocks formed in this way, making it a geologist's heaven and a site of scientific interest.

The Lodge's plant life is also rare and Charnwood Lodge is one of the few sites in Leicestershire and Rutland to host the lemon scented and hard ferns and the only place in the county to have an example of the alpine fungus *Melanoleuca evenosa*.

Nearby is Beacon Hill County Park near Loughborough, 135 hectares of grassland and woodland. It is a popular spot for walking and climbing, being the second highest point in Leicestershire at 248m.

The park contains a collection of native trees, first planted in 1996. Many of the trees are labelled, and there are several boxes that provide audio commentary on the biology and historical interest of selected tree species at the push of a button.

For rare plant life, the 9 hectares of Muston Meadows cannot be beaten. Muston is the finest lowland meadows in England and plays host to thirty-three types of grass and over 100 other species of flowering plant, most notably 10,000 green-winged orchids.

Dimminsdale, a former lead and limestone mine, has been reclaimed by natural heathland to form a paradise for rare species and areas of broadleaf woodland. The old mine pits form pools fed by nearby streams and the meadows are home to sheep, fescue, heath grass, heath bedstraw and harebell.

Other Conservation Sites, Parks and Nature Reserves

Lount Nature Reserve	Brocks Hill Park
Leighfield Forest	Market Bosworth Country Park
River Eye	Bradgate Park
Swithland Wood	Ashby Wolds Trail
Watermead National Park	Broombriggs Farm
River Mease	Donisthorpe Woodland Park
Charnwood Lodge	Melton Country Park
Burbage Common	Castle Hill Country Park
Fosse Meadows	Watermead Country Park

NATURAL PHENOMENON ...

Even today Leicestershire can be affected by the wonders of nature – from above and below.

Earthquakes

1750 was a year of earthquakes about the British Isles. At around noon on 30 September 1750, Leicestershire was affected by the strongest English earthquake of the year.

Although relatively mild in earthquake terms, the quivering earth caused some alarm. In Leicester, a rushing noise was heard and for a minute or two houses undulated, with chimneypots and slates thrown from the roofs. The only serious injury occurred to a child just outside the town, who was thrown from a chair into a fire and 'somewhat burnt'.

Meteor Storms

On 14 November 1866, Leicestershire was treated to a grand meteoric shower between midnight and 2 a.m. – or rather it would have been if it hadn't been so cloudy.

While in the south people gazed in wonder as the celestial rocks cascaded down to earth through clear skies, in Leicestershire it was a rather more dark and stormy occasion, although the veil of cloud and tempestuous conditions also added to the drama of the event. Gaps in the cloud allowed tantalising glimpses of the bright and 'very numerous' meteors, framed by flashes of lightning and driving rain as they descended to earth.

The countrywide phenomena was reported by *Illustrated London News* and *Symonds Monthly Metrological Magazine*.

On Christmas Eve 1965, Barwell and Earl Shilton were treated to a very special show of Christmas lights when the villages were showered with meteor fragments – with one the size of a Christmas turkey!

One meteorite went through a car, destroying the engine. When the owner of the car attempted to claim on his insurance, the company replied that it was an 'Act of God' and would not pay, so the man went to his local church to attempt to seek redress. He had no more luck with God than he did with the earthly authorities.

Rare Rainbows

The Smile in the Sky

In July 2011, the sky appeared to be literally smiling down on the residents of Market Bosworth when an upside down rainbow appeared above the town.

This 'smile in the sky' – or circumzenithal arc to give it its correct name – was not unknown but most unexpected, in Leicestershire at least. 'Circumzenithal arcs are seen relatively rarely in Britain because they can only be seen at the right combination of atmospheric conditions,' said a Met Office spokesperson.

So what are the right atmospheric conditions? Much colder than would be expected in July, certainly, as a circumzenithal arc is usually only found in polar regions!

Leicester's Rainbow Cloud

In February 2016, people across the county were amazed by an unusual phenomenon in the sky. An oval of bright rainbow-shaped light was observed above the county, described as a 'rainbow cloud'.

Leicester Mercury weatherman, Dave Mutton, explained that the cloud was the product of the meeting of a warm and cold front. This occurrence caused bits of the cloud to break up, with the resulting effect occurring in the break in the cloud cover. 'It is a very dramatic illustration of what happens when two different temperatures of air meet,' said Dave. 'Earlier in the day we had warmer air from the north-west, which produced a few showers. This air then met colder air which swept in.'

... AND UNNATURAL PHENOMENON

The Vardy Quake

In March 2016, Leicester City fans literally made the earth move at the King's Power Station when their joy caused an earthquake.

The fans were celebrating the Foxes' last-minute winning goal in a match against Norwich. At the time, a seismometer was in residence at the football ground, one of several planted by Leicester University as part of a scheme to measure earthquakes around the world.

In the final minutes of the match, instead of recording an earthquake caused by movements of the earth's crusts, the seismometer measured the fans making the earth move as their eruption of joy caused a quake, which measured at a magnitude of 0.3 – a minor earthquake!

'It wasn't just a case of cheering or clapping, it was 30,000 people standing up at the same time – an awful amount of energy,' said one of the researchers in explanation.

The 'earthquake' has been nicknamed 'The Vardy Quake' in honour of Leicester City's top scorer, Jamie Vardy.

2

TOWN AND COUNTRY

THE LIE OF THE LAND

Leicestershire is divided into seven distinct regions. These consist of three boroughs: Hinckley and Bosworth, Charnwood and Melton, and four districts: Oadby and Wigston, Blaby, Harborough and North West Leicestershire.

Boundaries and Borders
The boundaries of Leicestershire haven't changed much with time, probably because many are naturally determined. Since Saxon times, the northern border with Derbyshire has been marked by the River Trent. Here, the traditional crossing place between the two counties was established at King's Mill in 1009 by a charter of Ethelred the Unready.

Elsewhere, roads determine the county limits. Prehistoric Sewstern Lane is the long-established boundary between Leicestershire and Lincolnshire, dividing not only the two counties but also the village of Sewstern itself.

To the west, the Roman road of Watling Street divides Leicestershire from Warwickshire. Rutland was a part of Leicestershire briefly between 1974 and 1997: now Ermine Street acts as a divide between the two counties.

1

All Change

But towns as well as counties have moved in and out of Leicestershire. Snibson, and the area around Measham and Donisthorpe, used to be part of Derbyshire until they were moved in 1884 and 1897 as part of the Counties Act. The latter two towns were part of a swap: Leicestershire parted with Netherseal and Overseal as its part of the exchange.

Elsewhere, Leicestershire simply swallowed up parts of other counties. A burgeoning Market Harborough expanded so much that it encroached upon the Northamptonshire village of Little Bowden. The village's journey from one county to the other occurred slowly. In 1891, only part of the village was deemed to be in Leicestershire, but by 1927 the transition was complete.

THE SYMBOLS OF LEICESTERSHIRE

Leicestershire's coat of arms was granted on 25 January 1930. The arms are quartered to display the emblems of four important county families: the ermine cinquefoil of the Beaumont family, established by the first Norman earl, Robert de Beaumont; the double-tailed white lion of Simon de Montfort; the ermine plume of John of Gaunt, through whose son, Henry IV, Leicestershire passed into the royal estates; and finally the black sleeve of the Hastings family, landowners and prolific builders of castles.

But the importance of the countryside to Leicestershire is also reflected. Supporting the arms are a sheep and a black bull, representing the county's original industries of grazing and wool. Cresting the arms is a fox, representing the importance of fox-hunting to the county.

LEICESTERSHIRE'S POPULATION

The First People

Evidence suggests that the land that would become Leicestershire was occupied as early as the Palaeolithic period. Early habitation was small-scale and scattered. It seems that very early man was living and making stone tools on the banks of the River Bytham at Brooksby Quarry near Melton Mowbray as early as 950,000–450,000 years ago. Late Palaeolithic flint-knapping at Bradgate Park suggests that this area was also inhabited, however sporadically, possibly as a hunting camp.

The Welby Hoard

By the Bronze Age, it seems Leicestershire was attracting immigrants. The Welby Hoard was discovered in the late nineteenth century near to some of the major prehistoric routes that dissected and bisected Briton. The hoard consisted of axes, swords, a bowl and a bronze cauldron, all in a central European style unmatched anywhere else in Britain.

Although thought to be a scrap metal collection, the well-used weapons with their European design suggest they were deposited by people living locally who had come from elsewhere, rather than items from passing trade.

The Population Today

Today, we can say with greater certainty where the people of Leicestershire originate. The 2011 census shows the county had a total population of 650,489 people. Of this 578,432 were white British and 12,807 from other white groups.

In the city of Leicester, just over half of the population describe themselves as white British, compared to 80 per cent nationally – meaning Leicester just missed out on being the first British city with a minority white population.

The largest of Leicestershire's ethnic groups are Asian British, followed by other Asian groups, black British, Chinese, mixed white and Asian, mixed white and black.

Seventy per cent of Leicestershire's ethnic population live in an urban context, with 18 per cent on the fringes of cities or in towns and 12 per cent in villages. The urbanites are concentrated in the major settlements of Loughborough, Ashby de la Zouch, Market Harborough, Melton Mowbray, Oadby, Wigston and Lutterworth. Leicester is the main settlement of choice, largely because of the employment opportunities it offers.

Large-scale immigration began after Indian independence in the late 1940s. Ten million people became dislocated as tensions caused by the subsequent split of the subcontinent caused intercommunity violence. The British Nationality Act 1948 technically gave every commonwealth citizen the right to move to Britain, making it a natural choice for those seeking a refuge.

Britain also needed the workers, so many Indians and Pakistanis began to buy homes in Leicester's Spinney Hill and Belgrave areas where houses were most affordable.

But the 1970s saw the greatest influx when Idi Amin exiled all Asians in Uganda. Most of these immigrants settled in Leicester. Between 1968 and 1978, the city received 20,000 displaced Asian Africans, who again settled in the most affordable areas, namely around Highfields, Belgrave Road and Rushey Mead.

TOWNS AND VILLAGES

The First Towns

The first concrete evidence for substantial settlement in Leicestershire comes from the Neolithic period. Husbands Bosworth has the oldest scheduled monument in the county dating back to 3000 BC. The single-causewayed enclosure, complete with Late Neoloithic pottery and arrowheads discovered in its ditch, was probably a ritual site rather than a settlement. But in order to build and maintain it, organised groups of people had to be living nearby.

Evidence for Neolithic settlement does, however, exist at the other end of the county. Appleby possesses the remains of a substantial 6-acre enclosure containing several roundhouses surrounded by an oval ditch situated next to the River Mease. Miserton also displays ploughed-out enclosures or barrows dated to the early Neolithic era. But Croft has the earliest potential habitation site for this period, with the possible remains of postholes from houses dating to the late Mesolithic/early Neolithic period.

Evidence of an established, hierarchical society is suggested by the 250-300 suspected Bronze Age barrows in Leicestershire. The barrow cemetery near Lockington in north-west Leicestershire is one of the most impressive – if only for its gold hoard.

The hoard was found in the ditch of one of the barrows, although the mounds themselves are gone, identified only by crop marks. Its pottery vessels and copper dagger were accompanied by two bracelets made of thin sheet gold – some of the earliest examples of gold work in the British Isles.

Charcoal and charred bone found during excavations in the early 1990s suggest funerary activity in an earlier period, with the barrow built later over the remains. Clearly, Lockington was a sacred site of some long standing and would need to have been maintained by local settlements.

Examples of Bronze and Iron Age settlements can be found at Heather and Melton Mowbray. By now, Leicestershire was part of the tribal lands of the Corieltauvi, who occupied most of the east Midlands by the time of the Roman conquest.

But it is Leicestershire's hill forts that can be said to be its first towns. Centres of commerce and defence, they are, according to archaeologist Dr Jeremy Taylor, lecturer of Landscape Archaeology at the University of Leicester, 'the nearest thing to a town before places like Leicester ever existed.'

Situated along the ancient Salt Way, which runs from Winchester to the Humber, Beacon Hill's fort has natural defences that were supplemented with man-made ditches and banks.

Its close proximity to the road, and finds within the hill fort itself, suggest it was more than just a defensive site. A socketed axe, axe mold, a bronze bracelet and two spearheads found in a pit suggest a centre of production or trade which would have required long term, permanent occupation.

Five miles south of Melton, on the border with Warwickshire, Breedon Hill is Leicestershire's largest hill fort. Sadly largely destroyed by quarrying, pits, quern stones and postholes still remain, suggesting the site was occupied permanently for a lengthy period.

Seven miles south of Melton Mowbray is Burrough Hill and its single banked hill fort, the finest in Leicestershire and a centre of activity from the Neolithic period. The hill fort enjoyed its heyday in the Iron Age. It was well secured, with a defensive rampart that extended inwards as a tunnel leading to a double gateway and a guard chamber. Inside, there are signs of trade activities. But most significant of all, geophysical surveys by the School of Archaeology at Leicester University have identified roundhouses within the enclosure. Most unusual of all, it seems the hill was still occupied for the first century of the Roman period.

The Hallerton Hoard

It seems Leicestershire was in contact with Rome long before it sent its soldiers to conquer. The Hallerton Hoard is the largest hoard of British Iron Age coins – but it seems to have quite a few Roman ones too!

The hoard consisted of over 5,000 silver and gold coins, 4,835 minted by the Corieltauvi. But in amongst this native small change was Roman parade helmet jewellery and quite a few Roman coins. One, a silver denarius, dates to 211 BC – the oldest coin in Roman Britain.

Professor David Mattingly of Leicester University believes the hoard indicates contact between Leicestershire and Rome – before the lands of the Corieltauvi was conquered.

Ratae Corieltaurorum
When the legions finally arrived, they established what we recognise today as towns. One of them still survives under the modern name of Leicester. But to the Romans it was Ratae Corieltaurorum – 'the ramparts of the Corieltauvi'.

By the second century AD, Ratae was a model Roman town with bathhouses, grid pattern streets, temples, civic buildings and fine villas that spoke of a substantial *municipum* at the centre of the Romano-British trade route. The remains of its baths at Jewry Wall form the largest piece of standing Roman masonry in Britain.

But not every Roman town survived the test of time.

LOST PLACES

Fragments of lost Roman Leicestershire appear to tantalise from time to time. Upper Leighs at Drayton boasts the remains of a fine Roman villa complete with bathhouse and mosaic floors, as well as a rare silver and gold carnelian intaglio ring from the third century. At Ab Kettleby, the remains of a Roman villa's mosaic floor was discovered under the parish church, while remains of a Roman farm and temple at Appleby hint at a further unknown, unnamed town, now lost.

We can only guess at the lost settlements these buildings represent. But not all of Rome's lost places have mislaid their names...

Venonae

Between AD 43 and AD 409, Venonae was a thriving Roman town. The only written record of its name is preserved in the *Antonine Itinery*, a third-century travelogue for holidaying Roman emperors, which hints at Venonae's position by its distance from other Roman towns:

> **Iter II**, the route from Hadrian's Wall to Richborough in Kent, as **Venonis**, 12 miles from **Manduessedum** (Mancetter, Warwickshire) and 17 miles from **Bannaventa** (Whilton Lodge, Northhamptonshire).
>
> **Iter VI**, the route from London to Lincoln, again as **Venonis**, 8 miles from **Tripontium** (Cave's Inn, Warwickshire) and 12 miles from **Ratae** (Leicester, Leicestershire).
>
> **Iter VIII**, the route from York to London, once more as **Venonis**, again 12 miles from Leicester, though this time 18 miles from Whilton Lodge.

From this, we can deduce that Venonae was a station town, a resting point for travellers along the nearby Watling Street and Fosse Way. With the Roman evacuation of Britain, the traffic died and so did the town.

Today, Venonae's location is marked by the settlement of High Cross, near Wigston Parva. As for the town itself, all that remains are Roman coins, the stone foundations of its buildings, scattered tesserae from mosaic floors, roof tiles and the flues from long-gone central heating systems.

Tripontium

Situated in Sharwell, near Market Harborough, Tripontium lay to the west of Watling Street, the modern A5. Tripontium's position along a major road meant it was well connected to the main Roman road network of Britain.

The town was established as a military post soon after the Roman invasion of Britain in AD 47. Its name refers to the three bridges built over the River Avon and two of its tributaries at the town.

Tripontium prospered for 400 years before being abandoned in the fourth century AD. Its site has been continually excavated since 1961 by Rugby Archaeological Society, who soon realised that what they initially thought to be a small wayside settlement was something rather more when the remains of a sizable civilian town began to reveal itself, with large public bathhouses, an administrative building and a *mansio* or inn.

Temples and a forum are believed to still lie hidden but Tripontium has also revealed some unique finds such as a late Roman bronze belt buckle, adorned with early Christian symbols, and tiles covered in Latin graffiti referring to the Corieltauvi – the native Celtic tribe of the area – and a complete Roman alphabet.

But it is not just Roman settlements that are lost in Leicestershire.

Anebein

At the time of Domesday, Ambion Hill, which overlooks the battle site at Bosworth, was the site of a thriving country village called Anebein or Hanebein. But by the early fourteenth century the village was deserted, an early example of depopulation due to the ravages of the Black Death. With the people gone, the village fell into ruin. Local legend has it that when the forces of Richard III camped out the night before the Battle of Bosworth, they came across Anebein and found nothing but the ruined church. But those with a keener eye can still make out the ditch that surrounded the 160x180m extent of the village, as well as the remains of house platforms.

Elmesthorpe

Another victim of the plague was the village of Elmesthorpe or Aylmersthorpe, which had been continually inhabited from Roman times.

By 1297, Elmesthorpe was home to around forty to fifty farming families, but again the plague led to severe depopulation and as a result economic failure. People began to leave and the once prosperous farming village disappeared.

However, in 1710 people began to return – but not to the old village. Instead, they took the name but established their new settlement away from the site of old Elmesthorpe, the remains of which can still be seen from the new village church.

Ingarsby

Ingarsby is one of the best-preserved deserted medieval villages in England and a scheduled monument, 6 miles from Leicester and just north of Houghton on the Hill.

In 1086, thirty-two families were reported living in the village, but as time went on numbers dropped and by 1352 it was occupied by only a dozen families.

The village was finally lost in 1469 when Leicester Abbey enclosed the land and turned it over to sheep and cattle. All that remains of the once thriving settlement today are well defined rectangular mounds that were once houses and hollow track ways that define the village's lost streets and lanes.

Bradgate

Once there was a village in what is now Bradgate Park. The site of two houses are known, but it appears that the village was a scattered settlement rather than tightly packed around a central church. Perhaps this was why it was destroyed, as it would have been difficult to establish a deer park around such a dispersed settlement. But it may equally be because the owner of the land, Thomas Grey, did not want to be such near neighbours with his tenants when he began to build Bradgate House. Either way, the villagers were evicted and their homes destroyed. In 1500, Thomas Grey received a summons for depopulation. However, he was absolved as he claimed he had housed the displaced villagers elsewhere – which indeed he had. The new settlement was not too far away, at a ford near the River Lin. The settlement logically became known as the 'new town', which gradually evolved over time into its modern name, Newton Linford.

Alton and Knaptoft

Like Bradgate, Alton ceased to exist when the landowner decided the land could be put to better use. The village, which was situated between Coalville and Ashby, was turned into a monastic grange, with the land turned over to sheep rather than people. It was one of four villages deserted in Leicestershire for this reason, the others being Dishley, Ringlethorp and Weston.

Likewise Knaptoft was deserted in the seventeenth century when the land was enclosed for sheep farming. But it is not quite empty: some farm buildings and the church remain in use.

WHAT'S IN A NAME?

Bel the Giant

If local legends are to be believed, a doomed giant called Bel was responsible for the naming of at least four Leicestershire villages.

Bel was enjoying a drink with friends on a hill, when he drunkenly boasted he could make it to the town of Leicester in one leap. So he saddled up his sorrel mare and prepared to make the jump. The legend says the settlement on the hill was named Mount Sorrel to commemorate the start of his journey.

Bel cleared a mill and landed near the River Soar – but some distance from Leicester. This landing place was immortalised with the name 'one leap', which evolved into Wanlip.

Undeterred, Bel continued. But again he stopped short of his target – this time with such force that the landing broke the saddle girths. This earned the third settlement the name Birstall or 'burst all'.

Bel's final landing was the hardest by far. The plucky giant was thrown to the ground and stunned before his exhausted mare fell upon him, crushing the life out of him. And he still hadn't made it to Leicester.

Bel was buried where he fell, which explains the name of his final destination: Bel's Grave, later known as Belgrave.

The Griffin in the Well

Another legend claims that the hamlet of Griffydam near Worthington derived its name from its chalybeate well's unusual guardian.

The sacred spring in question was just off the main road of the village and jealously guarded by a griffin, until a local priest overcame it.

However, it seems that the true meaning of the village's name is more prosaic. It actually comes from 'Griffin's dam' for the pond and bank that can still be seen in the settlement.

There are other place names in Leicestershire that preserve the origins of settlements, or the origins of the people who have lived in them.

CELTIC PLACES

At least three Leicestershire settlements have their Celtic roots preserved in their names. Ratby and Ratcliffe upon Soar are both of Celtic origin, as evidenced by the inclusion of a variant of *ratae* in their names – the Celtic term for ramparts. Leicester is the other town. Although its name has changed, its original Roman name of Ratae Corieltaurorum also paid homage to its Celtic origins.

Such place names are rare now, as many of Leicestershire's settlements were renamed by later invaders.

SAXON INFLUENCES

The Saxons didn't always rename towns and villages, but they did like to leave their mark. Often, Saxon-occupied places ended with the suffix *ton* – the old Mercian term for a settlement. Examples include Thrussington, Syston and Cossington.

Other villages were renamed or founded with purely Saxon names. Great Bowdene is one of Leicestershire's oldest villages and derives its name from the Saxon female name Becga – making its meaning Becga's dun. Likewise Anstey in northern Leicestershire takes its name from the Angle term for a narrow forest track.

However, one particular word used in certain place names indicates that its residents were definitely not Saxon. Places like Walton on the Wold derive their name from the word *wealas*, the Saxon term for stranger. This was applied to places still settled by their original Romano-British inhabitants, demonstrating that not all the previous inhabitants of Leicestershire had been enslaved or driven away.

VIKING NAMES

Norse settlements can be recognised by the suffix *by* – the term for a farm or a settlement. Enderby, Oadby and Ingarsby are just three of the fifty-six place names in Leicestershire governed by this rule.

Ingarsby and Oadby also preserve another Viking naming tendency: that of naming settlements after their victorious war chiefs. Ingarsby is one of many places named after Ivar or Ingar the Boneless, one of the leading Viking lords. Oadby became Outi's dwelling after it was wrestled from the Saxons and Kirby Muxloe was named after Caeri, the Dane who founded it.

The Danes did not stop at settlements: they even took to renaming the landscape. The River Wreake took its name from the Danish term for 'twisted' while the Dane hills commemorate Leicestershire's whole period under the Dane Law.

Some place names combined Danish personal names suffixed with the Saxon *ton*. Thrussington, Syston, Cossington and Thurmaston are examples. Humberstone may also be one of these, possibly deriving its name from the Danish leader Ubba or Hubba, the first Viking to seize Leicester. But as with so many names, this is open to debate.

Other Saxon/Danish towns and villages in Leicestershire include:

Kegworth	From the Old English for 'key' or from the enclosure of a Dane called Kaggi or 'red Beard'.
Normanton le Heath	From the Old English for 'the settlement of northmen on the heath'. It was a village taken over or established by Norse or Danish settlers.
Measham	Originally known as Meas-Ham, meaning a settlement on the River Mease.
Ravenstone	The old Norse name *Hroefnes* and the suffix 'tun' suggests Ravenstone was an Anglo-Saxon village established by a Norseman called Hroefnes.
Melton Mowbray	The name Melton comes from the early English *Medeltone* meaning 'Middletown surrounded by small hamlets'. But Mowbray dates to Norman times and relates to the early Norman lords of the town.

THE NORMAN CONQUEST

The Normans were content to leave place names as they were –
unless they founded them or really wanted a reminder of home.
Newton Burgoland was originally known as Neutone or new
town of the Burgilon family, the settlement's Norman lords.
The name Mountsorrel, despite the claims of the legend of Bel,
almost certainly dates to this period, although the settlement it is
attached to existed much longer. It is thought to be named after
the French village Montsoreau where Henry II was buried.

On the other hand, Stretton en le Field seems to marry all
of Leicestershire's historical time periods into one. Although not
Roman in itself, it is one of the fifteen Strettons in England set
along a Roman road – hence the *stret/straet* element. The name is
also Saxon, hence the *ton* in the name and field or 'feld' relates to
the open country. 'En le' shows French influence.

GREAT HOUSES

One thing the Normans and their descendants were responsible
for was the founding of many of Leicestershire's great houses.

Belvoir Castle
Situated in the Vale of Belvoir, Belvoir Castle and the
vale it overlooks are named after the French for
'beautiful view'.

The castle also overlooks the villages of
Redmile, Woolsthorpe, Knipton, Harston,
Harlaxton, Croxton Kerrial and Bottesford
and Grantham. The local residents of these
settlements stubbornly refused to pronounce
the name in the same way as their French
overlords. Hence in Leicestershire, 'Belvoir'
is always pronounced 'beaver'.

Ashby de la Zouch Castle

In 1464, Edward IV granted the Norman manor house of Ashby to his Lord Chamberlain, Lord William Hastings. Hastings built an impressive four-storey tower castle there. But he did not live to enjoy it long as Richard III beheaded him in 1483.

However, Ashby de la Zouch Castle survived and played host to Henry VII, Mary, Queen of Scots and James and Charles I until the tower was partially destroyed by parliamentary forces in 1649.

Kirby Muxloe Castle

A manor house existed at Kirby Muxloe from the thirteenth century. But in 1480, the house became another of Lord William Hastings' building projects – and one he was doomed to never see through to completion.

Hastings planned to turn the manor house into a fortified castle, complete with towers, walls and a moat. The new construction was built strikingly from brick, which was expensive but was the new 'must have' building material for any late-medieval home improvements.

Perhaps Hastings wanted a fortified home because he was unsettled by the times. Unfortunately for him, his refuge remained incomplete when he met his untimely end.

The remaining Hastings family made the best of the half-finished castle and settled in its completed wing. But in the seventeenth century they abandoned Kirby Muxloe for better things. The castle was used as a farm and again abandoned, to fall into picturesque ruin.

Bradgate House

Bradgate House was also brick built and fortified. But unlike Kirby Muxloe Castle, it was completed before trouble struck its owners.

The house was constructed between 1499 and 1520. It was started by Thomas Grey, Marquis of Dorset and completed by his son. The finished house was 200m long and had two storeys.

A great hall and parlour lay at its core, with the family quarters in the east wing and the service areas in the west.

Bradgate was home to Lady Jane Grey during her childhood and remained in the Grey family until the twentieth century. However, the family abandoned the house during the eighteenth century when they made their chief residence in Staffordshire.

INDUSTRIAL TOWNS AND VILLAGES

The Industrial Revolution brought about its own changes to Leicestershire, with villages growing up in response to the new industries – and new towns arising altogether.

Whitwick

Whitwick began as a medieval village, listed in the Domesday Book, complete with castle and annual country fairs. It is unique in that it is the only village in England to contain three cities. The City of Three Waters and the City of Dan are legitimate postal addresses within the village. But the third city's name and location is somewhat elusive. Some locals maintain it is the City of Hockley, while others refer to it simply as 'Hockley'. Its location is vaguer still, with no one being exactly sure where it is, although others speculate it is near to the parish church.

Until the nineteenth century, the village's only industry was framework knitting, but the blossoming of the mining industry transformed the village into a mining town. The old village's buildings, with few exceptions, were swept away and replaced by Victorian red brick housing.

Coalville

At the beginning of the nineteenth century, Coalville didn't exist. Instead, the land it would occupy was covered with brambles and gorse with a country track called Long Lane running down its centre.

Then William Stenson sunk a deep mineshaft on the land and the rest is history. The Whitwick Colliery grew up around the shaft – and Coalville grew up around the mine. It started in 1824 with a few miners' cottages running down Long Lane. But by 1834, the railway had reached the town and 'Coalville', as it was now known, became linked to Leicester, allowing it to expand its interests into textiles and engineering.

The town did not acquire its name from the mineral that gave birth to it, but from the name of Stenson's large house, which he built nearby from the proceeds of his mine.

Swannington and Coleorton

Swannington had been a mining village from the sixteenth century – on a small scale at least, with villagers taking advantage of the exposed coal layers in the area, gathering coal from the nearby fields.

But it took the advent of the Leicester and Swannington Railway for the village mines to really develop. The ease of transporting coal from the village meant the mines expanded, in turn attracting miners from other areas, leading to massive house building.

But with the growth of Coalville, many miners left equally as quickly, leaving Swannington's mining industry to quietly decline. Today, it is a pleasant commuter village.

Like Swannington, Coleorton was a mining village from the fifteenth century. By the 1420s, it had gained a sufficient reputation for its coal to exchange its original name of Overton Saucy for that of Coal Overton, later shortened to its present form.

The village was the birthplace of William Stenson, who expanded mining in the area. So it appears that in more ways than one, Coleorton was key to mining in Leicestershire.

BEST AND WORST

The Sixth Happiest Place in the UK

Blaby is the sixth happiest place in the UK, according to the Office of National Statistics' annual wellbeing survey for 2014/15. The *Leicester Mercury* reported that the town is the only place in the Midlands to make the top ten in the poll. Good walks, parks and canals, coupled with friendly people and a close community spirit are cited as Blaby's main attractions by its locals – as well as the 450 clubs and organisations in the area that keep them occupied.

The Most Desirable Place to Live

According to a Royal Mail survey in 2015, Wigston is the most desirable place to live in Leicestershire. The town won out against its nearest competitors Newton Linford, Loughborough, Kibworth and Mountsorrel because of its affordable housing, transport links and green spaces.

The Best Place to Bring Up Children

Quorn is one of the top five places in the UK to bring up children. According to the *Leicester Mercury*, this is because the village offers 'the peace and space that all children thrive on'. The tranquil countryside is also safe, as Quorn's crime rate is low – and the village itself offers excellent schools.

The Worst Place in England to Raise a Family

In 2016, however, Leicester was named the worst place in England to raise a family. The *Leicester Mercury* reported how the Uswitch Better Family Life Index had analysed thirty-three elements of family life across 138 council areas in Britain including pay, GCSE grades, weather, childcare and access to doctors. The survey claimed the city had fewer primary schools, high council tax, the fourth worst employment level in the UK – and that 43 per cent of Leicester parents were worried they weren't giving their children the best start in life.

But Sir Peter Soulsby, the city's mayor, dismissed the report as having no basis in fact. Instead, he accused Uswitch of 'a cheap bit of marketing' to draw attention to its comparison site services.

Others agreed, with local MPs such as John Ashworth defending the city's play areas and children's festivals. 'We have two young children who we are raising in the city,' he said, 'and it is a great place.'

3

MOVERS AND SHAKERS

Many people have helped shape Leicestershire and make it the great county it is. Likewise, Leicestershire has produced many people who have helped shape the world.

LOCAL LORDS

John of Gaunt

John of Gaunt was Earl of Leicester as well as Lancaster. He was also the son, brother, uncle and father of kings.

Leicester Castle was reputedly one of his favourite seats. At his death in 1399, his estates passed on to his son, Henry Bollingbrook. Bollingbrook's cousin, Richard II, had exiled him, so his newly inherited estates were forfeit. But on his father's death, Henry returned to reclaim his inheritance – and ousted his cousin from the throne, seizing it for himself.

As Henry IV, Henry's inheritance – which included the whole of Leicestershire – became part of the royal estates.

Richard III

On 14 August 1483, Richard III wrote a letter to the King of France 'from my castle in Leicester'. It was the last recorded occupation of the castle by one of its owners.

On his last, fateful visit to Leicester, Richard did not stay in his castle, as it was by then too rundown. Instead, he stayed in Leicester's plush White Boar Inn and the rest, as they say, is history. But by fighting the last battle of the War of the Roses in Leicestershire and becoming the last monarch to die in combat on British soil, he put the county firmly on the map of British history.

Richard also managed to be ignobly buried and then lost for centuries. But that also worked in Leicestershire's favour, for his rediscovery in 2012 and subsequent reburial in Leicester Cathedral in 2015 has led the county to become a major tourist hotspot, increasing the local economy in 2015 by 6.6 per cent and leading to the creation of 1,800 new jobs.

Simon de Montfort

Simon de Montfort was Leicestershire's sixth earl from 1239 until his untimely death and dismemberment at the Battle of Evesham in 1265.

De Montfort was a major mover and shaker in medieval England. He married Eleanor, the sister of Henry III, and then turned on his brother-in-law, leading the Second Baron's War in 1264 and becoming the *de facto* ruler of Britain.

De Montfort is also credited with calling two famous parliaments in 1264. The first, held in the great hall of Leicester Castle, stripped the king of his unlimited authority. Four knights from every county in England were called to attend.

But the second parliament, held between January and March 1265, involved ordinary citizens for the first time. As well as knights, two burgesses from each town were summoned. Thus de Montfort was one of the first advocates of the modern parliamentary system.

In Leicestershire itself, de Montfort improved matters for its people by introducing inheritance by primogeniture instead of ultimogeniture (inheritance by the youngest child). This Leicestershire custom had been impoverishing the county's estates and businesses as, in practice, it meant splitting inheritances amongst all the deceased's offspring. Primogeniture left the deceased estate intact and safe in the hands of the eldest child.

But one of de Montfort's most shameful acts was to expel the Jews from Leicester in 1231, 'for the good of my soul and the souls of my ancestors and successors.' The expulsion wasn't so much an act of anti-Semitism as a calculated attempt to win the favour of the people of Leicestershire. Banishing the Jews effectively freed the people of debt, as Jews were the only ones who could practice usury.

However, de Montfort's scheme backfired. The Jews didn't go very far. For despite being earl, de Montfort didn't own the whole county. The other half belonged to his great-aunt, Margret, Countess of Winchester, a fact de Montfort bitterly disputed. The countess probably offered the Jews sanctuary to score points against her great-nephew.

The Greys of Groby

The Greys of Groby were notable, if not notorious, for their links to the Crown. That link was first established when John Grey of Groby married Elizabeth Woodville. John died leaving Elizabeth near destitute with two young sons. A chance encounter with King Edward IV eventually led to their marriage.

Elizabeth's daughter, the half-sister of Thomas and Richard Grey, later married Henry Tudor who became Henry VII. But a few generations later, the Greys links to the Crown were further strengthened by the marriage of Francis, the granddaughter of Henry VIII's favourite sister, Mary, to Henry Grey, the Earl of

Suffolk. Their daughter, Lady Jane Grey, the tragic nine-day queen, grew up on the Greys' estate at Bradgate Park.

Henry VIII's will stipulated that if his own children died without issue, the crown was to pass to his sister Mary's descendants – leaving out the Scottish royal family descended from his elder sister Margaret.

After Edward V's premature death in 1553, unscrupulous nobles sought to raise their own profile by manipulating the will. Edward was persuaded to make his cousin Jane his heir, over his sisters Mary and Elizabeth. Jane was married to Guildford Dudley, the son of the Duke of Northumberland, and declared queen.

Mary joined her younger sister Elizabeth and, with the help of a popular uprising, regained the support of the Privy Council. Jane and her husband were arrested after just nine days.

Jane's life may have been spared if, during her time of imprisonment in the Tower of London, Sir Thomas Wyatt had not led a protest against the return of Catholicism – which was joined by Jane's father. As Jane remained a threat as a focus for future Protestant revolts, she was eventually executed in 1554.

After this, the Greys' relationship with the Crown soured. Not only did the family forfeit their barony because of Henry Grey's rebellion, but Elizabeth I also overturned her father's will in favour of the surviving Grey sisters by instead naming James IV of Scotland as her heir.

Perhaps this explains the stance taken by the family during the English Civil War: Thomas Grey, Lord Grey of Groby and MP for Leicester, fought on the side of Parliament and in 1649 was the only aristocratic signatory on the death warrant of Charles I.

REBELS AND POLITICIANS

Thomas Skeffington
Skeffington was High Sheriff of Leicestershire from 1575–76, 1587–89 and 1598–99. He saw to it that Leicestershire did its bit

for queen and country by calling upon the county's men to take up arms and defend the nation from the threat of the Spanish Armada.

Some 12,530 men were raised, with 2,000 sent to guard Tilbury Docks while the rest trained in combat in case of invasion.

Sir Everard Digby

Everard Digby was born around 1576 in Leicestershire to a wealthy landowning family, whose properties included Donington le Heath Manor.

But Digby was also a secret Catholic convert at a time when the faith was under attack. And so, in 1605, despite his popularity at court and being knighted by James I, Digby became part of the Gunpowder Plot, financing and directing from behind the scenes.

If the plan to blow up Parliament had been successful, he would have been one of the leading players in raising a rebellion in the Midlands. Instead, on its failure, he was captured at Holbeche House near Dudley and despite being the only plotter to plead guilty, was hung, drawn and quartered on 30 January 1606.

George Villiers

George Villiers was the son of a local Leicestershire landowner who did very well with the Crown and advanced his family into the aristocracy.

Born in 1592, to the second wife of Sir George Villiers of Brooksby Hall near Melton Mowbray, George was the third son and so had no great expectations. But his mother introduced him at court and there in 1614 he quickly caught the eye of the first Stuart king, James I.

James's behaviour with Villiers was an open scandal, with the king openly hugging and kissing the young knight. Whether or not these scandalous feelings were reciprocated is uncertain, but George was quickly promoted, becoming first a baron, then a marquis, then an earl, the Duke of Buckingham, and in 1619 Lord High Admiral – despite his lack of prowess in the field.

George remained in favour with James's son, Charles I. But he had earned the hatred of the Puritans and Parliament because of his military disasters. He was assassinated at breakfast in 1628, on his way to a further expedition in France. His assassin, an officer called John Felton, declared he killed Villiers because he had 'for so long gone unpunished for his crimes.'

Henry Smith and John Cook

Henry Smith was born in Withcote in 1620. He studied law at Oxford and went on to become a Member of Parliament for Leicestershire in 1640.

In 1649, Smith sat as a commissioner for the High Court of Justice at the trial of Charles I. His was the nineteenth signature on the death warrant of the king.

After the Restoration, Smith was tried for regicide and sentenced to death. But using his legal prowess, he successfully appealed his sentence, which was commuted to life imprisonment. Smith was committed to the Tower of London until 1664 when he was transported to Jersey, where he died at Mont Orgueil Castle.

John Cook was not so lucky. Born in Burbage in 1608, he too left Leicestershire to study law, eventually becoming Solicitor General of the Commonwealth of England.

Cook was in many ways a progressive lawyer. He established a prisoner's right to silence and advocated many reforms to the law, including the abolition of imprisonment for debt, and restrictions on the death penalty for those convicted of theft. Cook recognised that many of those who stole did so out of desperation and campaigned for probation, rather than hanging in such cases.

Cook was not an anti-monarchist, but when Charles I began to buck the law, he joined those who tried the king for treason. He led the prosecution, so helping condemn Charles to death. Unlike many, at the Restoration he stood by his actions. Shortly before his death, he wrote to his wife: 'We fought for the public good and would have enfranchised the people and secured the welfare of the whole groaning creation, if the nation had not more delighted in servitude than in freedom.'

He was hung, drawn and quartered on 16 October 1660.

Alice Hawkins

Many local Leicestershire women played a significant role in the fight for women's suffrage. One of the most prominent and remarkable was Alice Hawkins.

Alice was born in 1863 and lived most of her life in Leicester. Unlike many others in the movement, she was working class, a shoe machinist by trade. She was politically active from her teens, and became keenly aware that women in her industry had inferior pay and conditions to their male counterparts.

In 1907, she attended her first meeting of the Women's Social and Political Union (WSPU) in Hyde Park, London. That very day, she became active in the movement. Her first spell in prison for her political activities quickly followed. Over the next seven years, she was jailed five times, serving terms in Holloway and Leicester prisons.

After her first sentence was complete, Alice invited Sylvia Pankhurst to speak at Leicester and shortly afterwards the Leicester branch of the WSPU was formed. Alice was the trailblazer – the only one to mount platforms to speak and the only woman to challenge future Prime Minister Winston Churchill when he spoke in Leicester.

She died in Leicester in 1946 aged 83.

Thomas Babington

Thomas Babington was MP for Leicester from 1800–18, and a leading Anglican evangelical. Educated at St John's College, Cambridge, he worked closely with William Wilberforce on social improvement and the famous bills to abolish the slave trade. Wilberforce and Babington spent much time at Babington's Rothley retreat working on the text of the bills, and on the analysis of the Select Committee's enquiries into the trade.

BENEVOLENT BENEFACTORS

William Wyggeston

Wyggeston was a successful wool merchant and Mayor of Leicester in 1448–49 and 1459–90. He also represented Leicester in the seventh parliament of Henry VII.

Towards the end of his life in 1500, Wyggeston dedicated a portion of his wealth from the income of his Swannington estate to establishing a hospital for the care of the elderly poor. The hospital was set up on land near to Leicester Cathedral.

Wyggeston's motives may not have been totally altruistic as it was common in the medieval period for wealthy men to undertake good works for the benefit of their soul. But Wyggeston's legacy endured. Although the original building is gone, the Wyggeston Hospital continues today, but as a retirement home for the elderly on Hinckley Road.

Wyggeston's contribution to the wellbeing of Leicester's poor is recognised by the inclusion of his figure on Leicester's clock tower.

Leicester's Hospital.

After Wyggeston's death, his son Thomas continued in his father's benevolent footsteps by using part of his inheritance to establish a grammar school in Leicester. This in turn bequeathed its name to the later Wyggeston Grammar School for Boys, which survives now as Wyggeston and Queen Elizabeth I College.

Robert Smyth

Market Harborough's own version of Dick Whittington left the town to seek his fortune in 1570. He found work as an archivist with the Lord Mayor of London and eventually became the Chief Comptroller of the City of London.

But Smyth never forgot his roots. He regularly sent money back to his home town to provide bread for the 'godly, honest poor' and set up the grammar school in the town, which remained open from 1614 until 1909.

Henry Fearson

The vicar of All Saints' church, Loughborough, campaigned to bring clean water to the town. When he died in 1885, people lined the streets of Loughborough in respect.

Dr John Charles Bucknill and John Buck

Dr Bucknill was born in 1817 at Market Bosworth. After learning of work at the Hanwell Asylum in Middlesex, where patients went without restraints, he became convinced that insanity was a brain disease that could be treated with medication.

Bucknill began to promote and support the practice as well as promote the civil rights of patients. His work laid the foundations for the more humane treatment of patients in asylums.

In 1853, John Buck resigned his position as part-time medical officer with Leicestershire Borough Police to become super-intendent of the Leicestershire and Rutland County Lunatic Asylum near Victoria Park.

Buck reformed the prison-like environment of the institution, persuading the asylum commissioners to build a washhouse, a bakery, chapel, recreation hall, workshops and farm buildings – to service the asylum and provide the inmates with therapeutic employment opportunities. He also instigated regular excursions for the patients and a brass band.

Thomas Fielding Johnson

Some sixty-three years later, the asylum was no more. Businessman and philanthropist Thomas Fielding Johnson bought up and donated the site for the establishment of Leicester's own university college, later Leicester University. The old asylum building, now the university's administrative block, was named in his honour.

Charles Bennion

Although not a native of Leicestershire, Charles Bennion made his fortune from engineering in the county and made it his home. In 1925, he found a way to show the people of Leicestershire just how great his regard was.

That year, the 850-acre Bradgate estate was put up for sale by the Grey family. They had offered it to the people of Leicestershire for public use, but the money to buy the land was not available to the borough. So Mr Bennion stepped in. He purchased the parkland and, after placing it in trust, formally presented it to the people of Leicestershire as a somewhat late Christmas gift on 29 December 1928.

INTELLECTUALS, SCIENTISTS AND ENGINEERS

Henry Bates

Born on 8 February 1825, Bates self-educated himself in natural history before leaving Leicestershire for the Amazon, where he remained for eleven years, periodically sending home new specimens. In all, Bates posted back 14,712 species – 8,000 new to science at the time.

But Bates's crucial discovery was that of mimicry in animals. He discovered that hoverflies would imitate the warning noises of wasps and bees to defend themselves against danger. The discovery was named 'Batesian Mimicry' in his honour.

Thomas Simpson

Thomas Simpson was born at Market Bosworth in 1710. The son of a weaver, a craft he himself took up in his free time, he taught himself mathematics.

In 1743, Simpson graduated from weaving by day and teaching by night to becoming a full-time mathematician when he was awarded a post at the Royal Military Academy in Woolwich. He became a Fellow of the Royal Society and is attributed with the invention of 'Simpson's Rule', a formula for estimating the area under a curve.

His works include *The Nature and Laws of Chance* and *The Doctrine of Annuities and Reversions.*

Sir Frank Watson Dyson

Born in 1868, this Measham Astronomer Royal was noted as an authority on the spectrum of the corona and chromosphere of solar eclipses – and the invention of radio pips. In 1919, during an expedition to observe solar eclipses in South America, he also confirmed Einstein's Theory of Relativity of the effect of gravity on light.

T.E.R. Philips

Born in Kibworth in 1868, this Anglian cleric turned his eyes to the heavens in more than the spiritual sense. During his tenure as a curate and vicar in the South of England, Philips became an amateur astronomer, with the surface currents of Mars and Jupiter his particular interest.

His expertise was soon recognised and Philips became director of the Jupiter section of the British Astrological Society from 1900–33. Between 1935 and 1940, he branched out to include Saturn in his Society activities. Philips became president of the Royal Astrological Society from 1927–29 and won the Jackson-Gwilt medal of the Royal Astronomical Society in 1918.

Sir Nicholas Ridley

Sir Nicholas Harold Lloyd Ridley, inventor of intraocular lenses, was born in Kibworth in 1906. An eye surgeon and consultant, Ridley treated Royal Air Force casualties with eye injuries in the Second World War. He noticed that those with splinters of acrylic plastic from cockpit canopies lodged in their eyes did not have the same inflammatory reaction as those with glass splinters. This led Ridley to develop artificial Perspex lenses to treat cataracts and on 29 November 1949 he performed the first implant of an intraocular lens.

It was not until 1950 that he left a lens permanently in the eye. Although it took until 1981 for the technique to be widely regarded as safe and effective, cataract extractions using intraocular lens transplants are now the most common form of eye surgery.

Frank Whittle

Whittle, the inventor of the jet engine, developed some of the world's first jet planes at the British Thomson-Houston works in Lutterworth during the late 1930s and '40s. The engine for the UK's first jet airplane, the Gloster E.28/39, was produced in Lutterworth under his direction.

EXPLORERS AND ADVENTURERS

Charles Throsby

Charles Throsby was born in Glenfield in 1771, but he made his name much further afield. In 1802, he departed Portsmouth as surgeon on a convict transport to Sydney, Australia. The voyage was smooth and it was reported none of the male convicts under Throsby's care died.

Throsby settled in the colony, acting as magistrate, and was employed as a surgeon and superintendent. But after a brief return visit to England in 1817, he returned to Australia for good and began exploring of his adopted homeland.

On 8 March 1818, he set out as part of an exploratory group seeking a route to Jervis Bay. Three weeks later, Throsby's section of the party arrived at their destination via the Kangaroo and Lower Shoalhaven rivers. They beat their companions to their destination by asking a pair of passing Aborigines for directions!

Further expeditions followed. In 1819, Throsby pioneered explorations to the west of the Blue Mountains. The rich, fertile land was to be a boon to future settlers and Throsby himself was awarded a parcel at Bong Bong near Moss Vale.

Later, Throsby was put in charge of road construction to the Goulburn planes, during which time he reached the Yass river and the Murrumbidgee river – again, after talking to the Aborigines.

HISTORIANS, ACADEMICS AND WRITERS

John Throsby

The first historian to write a full history of Leicestershire was born on 21 December 1740 in the city of Leicester to alderman Nicholas Throsby and his wife.

John began work as the parish clerk at St Martin's church in Leicester and this gave him the perfect opportunity to begin his studies into the county of his birth. His *Memories of the Town and County of Leicester* contained his own drawings. He was also careful only to include descriptions of sights and events which he had witnessed or had been witnessed by people he interviewed.

Throsby also took a keen interest in local archaeology, as shown by his *Letter to the Earl of Leicester on the Recent Discovery of the Roman Cloaca at Leicester, with Some Thoughts on the Jewry Wall.* He was made a freeman of Leicester in 1760.

In addition he was also a great admirer of Richard III, who he viewed as 'one of the greatest heroes England has ever produced' – a view that has only begun to be shared by many other people in recent times.

Throsby was a trailblazer for the local historians who followed after him. John Nichols described him in his *History and Antiquities of Leicestershire* as 'a man of strong natural genius, who, during the vicissitudes of a life remarkably chequered, rendered himself conspicuous as a draughtsman and topographer.'

Anna Barbauld

Anna Laetitia Barbauld (*née* Aikin, 1743–1823) was a poet, essayist and innovative children's author born in Kibworth Harcourt. Thanks to her father, John Aikin, she had a classical education denied to many women of the time. Her writings – at a time when it was rare for women to have any sort of successful writing career – also entered the political sphere.

Initially famous for her poems, she later published *Miscellaneous Pieces in Prose* with her brother, leading many to compare her to Samuel Johnson. After a period teaching in a school with her husband, Barbauld began her most radical political writings during the French Revolution.

When the law granting dissenters full citizenship was defeated in 1790, she wrote *An Address to the Opposers of the Repeal of the Corporation and Test Acts.* She also supported William Wilberforce's anti-slavery stance and, after the defeat of his 1791 attempt to abolish the slave trade, she published her *Epistle to William Wilberforce Esq. on the Rejection of the Bill for Abolishing the Slave Trade* as a show of solidarity.

Barbauld's poetry laid the foundation of British romanticism but she fell out of favour in 1812 when she published *Eighteen*

Hundred and Eleven, a criticism of Britain's involvement in the Napoleonic Wars, and was so shocked at its reception that she never wrote again.

Bernard Newman

Born in 1897 in Ibstock, Newman was a historian, an expert on spies – and the great-nephew of the author George Eliot. He wrote over 100 books of fiction and non-fiction, covering his main areas of interest: travel and politics, mysteries, science fiction and children's books.

Newman's interest in spying stemmed from the First World War, when he was sent undercover to Paris because of his fluency in French. After the war, he became a civil servant but also an avid traveller, visiting over sixty countries before 1939, as well as lecturing across Europe – even meeting Hitler. He witnessed the invasion of France by the Germans and on his return to England joined the Ministry of Information and began writing patriotic novels. He was also sent to the USA to garner American support for the British cause.

These activities, plus his well-informed writings, led to suggestions that he was a British spy. His novel *Spy Catcher* was praised as one of the best books on espionage.

Claire Hollingworth

Born in 1911 in the village of Knighton, Hollingworth was a journalist and war correspondent. On 31 August 1939, she was in Poland on an assignment from the *Daily Telegraph* to report on growing tensions in Europe.

While driving along the Polish-German border, Hollingworth noticed a massing of German tanks and troops. Realising that she was witnessing a gathering invasion force, she called the British Embassy in Warsaw the next morning. The Embassy was unconvinced – so Hollingworth hung her phone out of the window so they could hear the German troops.

Hollingworth was not only one of the first people to witness the outbreak of war – but also the first journalist to report it.

OTHER LEICESTERSHIRE LITERARY FIGURES

Sue Townsend   The late author of the Adrian Mole books was born and bred in Leicester. A lifelong socialist, Townsend's political beliefs influenced many of her books and plays.

Colin Wilson   Another Leicester writer, Wilson was the author of *The Outside* and associated with the 'angry young men' movement of the 1960s.

C.P. Snow CBE   The novelist and physicist was born in Leicester and educated at what is now the University of Leicester.

Frederick Thorpe   Thorpe was the publisher behind Ulverscroft large print books, which were produced to help those with failing eyesight to keep on reading. The name for his publishing house came from the old Augustine priory near his farm in Leicestershire.

Joe Orton   Leicester-born playwright and author whose literary style was best described as 'Ortonesque', so particular were his cynical black comedies. Orton was murdered by his partner Kenneth Halliwell in 1967.

Many famous literary figures have also passed through Leicestershire. **Samuel Johnson**, the famous essayist and lexicographer, worked very briefly as a teacher at Dixie Grammar, after he prematurely left Oxford because of debt. However, Johnson's post did not last long and he quit after only four months because he was unable to tolerate the 'boorish' 4th baronet.

Poet laureate **Philip Larkin** lived in Leicester in the 1940s, when he worked at Leicester University library. While in the town, he wrote thirteen poems. His last address in the city, on Dixon Drive, provided the surname for Kingsley Amis's hero Jim Dixon, the eponymous hero of *Lucky Jim*.

ARTISTS AND CRAFTSPEOPLE

Mary Linwood
Born in Birmingham in 1755, Mary Linwood was a famous needlework artist who made Leicester her home. She moved to the town in 1764 when her wine merchant father became bankrupt and her mother opened a boarding school for young ladies. Mary took over the school and continued to run it for fifty years. Simultaneously, however, she was making a name for herself as an embroidery artist. By the age of 31, she was mixing with royalty, exhibiting her work to Queen Charlotte at Windsor Castle.

Over her lifetime Mary produced over 100 pictures, many of which were full-sized copies of Old Masters. She met most of the crowned heads of Europe and exhibited in Russia, where Catherine the Great tried to buy her whole collection for £40,000. Mary refused, as she wanted her work to stay in England. One piece, however, was purchased: a copy of a painting by the Italian artist Salvatore Rosa, which sold for more than the original.

Mary also created her own designs such as the 'Judgment of Cain' and a portrait of Napoleon, for which he awarded her the Freedom of Paris in 1803.

John Flower

Known as 'The Leicester Artist', Flower was a landscape and architectural artist born in Leicester in 1793.

Initially apprenticed to a framework knitter, Flower's talent for drawing was noticed by a local doctor who gave him art lessons. Mary Linwood eventually became his patron and it was she who arranged for him to study art in London.

On his return to Leicester, Flower began to teach art and paint landscapes. His work was very much concentrated around Leicestershire, although he did branch out to neighbouring counties. In 1826 he published *Views of Ancient Buildings in the Town and County of Leicester*. He remained in the town until his death in 1861, in the home he and the architect Henry Goddard had designed on Upper Regent Road.

Ernest Gimson

Gimson was born in Leicester in 1864, the son of Josiah Gimson, the owner of the Vulcan works and founder of Gimson & Co. Ernest was apprenticed to a Leicester architect at the age of 18, but when he attended a lecture on arts and socialism given by William Morris at the Leicester Secular Society, he became inspired.

That night, he talked with Morris until two in the morning, the beginning of a long-standing association. Once his architectural education was complete, Gimson moved to London, armed with letters of recommendation from Morris. There, he began to develop his own style, using naturalistic details, flowers, animals and natural textures. After travelling, he joined Morris's Society for the Protection of Ancient Buildings and moved to the Cotswolds to found an artisan community, experimenting in furniture design.

Many of Gimson's buildings can still be seen around Leicestershire. They include Inglewood and the white house in Stoneygate, and Lea, Stoneywell and Rockyfield cottages in Charnwood.

He died in 1919 and was described by the critic Nikolaus Pevsner as 'the greatest of the English architect-designers'.

LOCAL CHARACTERS

Daniel Lambert was one of the largest humans that ever lived – but he didn't start out that way. Until his mid-twenties, he was tall and well built but not overweight. He swam regularly, even teaching local children, and ate a moderate diet, drinking only water.

Then, for no explicable reason, he began to balloon until, by the age of 35, he had reached 53 stone. Unable to continue in his role as gaoler of Leicester Prison, Lambert briefly moved to London where he made a living from being 'visited' by gawpers at his house. But he quickly returned home, where he died at the age of 39 after visiting Stamford Races.

Joseph Merrick, nicknamed the Elephant Man, was born in Leicester in 1862, in the slum area of Wharf Street. He was a normal child until at 21 months growths began to appear on his body – including one that resembled an elephant's trunk across his mouth. Soon after, his mother died and Joseph, rejected by his father, was left to fend for himself. Unable to find employment, he was forced into Leicester Workhouse for three years until in 1882 he joined a freak show.

In London, Frederick Treves, a doctor at the Royal London Hospital, spotted Merrick. Merrick took up residence at the hospital after a tour of Belgium and remained there until he died in 1890.

4

WORKING LIFE

MAJOR EMPLOYERS

Leicestershire folk have been employed in a diverse number of industries over the centuries …

Quarrying

Quarrying was one of Leicestershire's earliest industries. The geology of the county makes it to this day a rich source of rock, with the hard, igneous rocks of north-west Leicestershire especially important.

Stone from Quorn has been quarried for millstones since the Iron Age and the Romans transported it to build Roman Leicester. No wonder the village's name means 'the hill where the millstones are quarried'.

From Roman times, slate was also important to villages like Swithland, who maintained a trade in the material right the way through to the nineteenth century. Swithland stone was converted for roof tiles and more unusually, gravestones, due to its rough texture and easy of carving.

Charnwood's hard igneous rocks were much sought after for whetstones and quernstones and even today the granite quarries of Bardon Hill, Breedon Hill and Whitwick are an important source of crushed aggregate, which is transported about the country. The pink granite of Mountsorrel has also been prized since the eighteenth century.

Farming

As with most places, agriculture was a mainstay of the Leicestershire economy up until the Industrial Revolution. Sheep and cattle were the most common commodities, as Leicestershire's heavy clay soils are still hard work for growing crops.

After 1650, livestock farming became more common as grain prices fell and the profits for wool and dairy began to rise. But British livestock, like the now extinct Forest Sheep of Charnwood, were generally small and not known for the quality of their meat.

Then, in the eighteenth century, an agricultural revolution occurred in Leicestershire. Farmer Robert Bakewell of Dishley near Loughborough began to pioneer selective breeding. His experiments resulted in two new types of livestock: the Longwool Sheep and Longhorn Cattle. Both were the cornerstones for the future of meat and wool across Leicestershire and England. Longwool Sheep, now a heritage breed and the ancestor of many later breeds such as the English Leicester, the Border Leicester, Bluefaced Leicester, Scotch Mule and Welsh Halfbreed, produced excellent wool and mutton while Longhorn Cattle are esteemed even today for their meat and milk.

The Wool and Hosiery Industry

But even before Robert Bakewell's agricultural breakthrough, wool was a major part of Leicestershire's economy, from the Middle Ages onwards. Shepshed was one village noted for its sheep farming and wool production. Indeed its name may well mean 'hill where sheep graze'.

Well Yard on Forest Street was once known as the 'Wool Yard'. This was the place where merchants gathered to buy Shepshed wool. Buyers would come from as far afield as Bradford and the abbey that owned the village and its farmland had permission to sell to merchants from Flanders. Shepshed's role in the wool trade remained important up until 1811.

But agriculture never paid well and so it became common to supplement the farm labouring families' incomes with hand-knitting. This cottage industry dominated in the south and east of Leicestershire until the end of the seventeenth century.

In the Tudor era, two changes occurred. In 1589, the first stocking frame was invented. There was also a change in men's fashion; the long robes of the medieval period were replaced by the doublet and hose. This meant the legs were on show, making the stocking a fashion item in its own right, rather than just an undergarment.

The first stocking frame in Leicestershire was in Hinckley. It was set up in 1640 by William Illiffe in his own house for £60. Illiffe started a trend and soon stocking workers across the county were working from home on rented frames. In 1720, Daniel Defoe noted:

> Leicester is an ancient, large and populous town … they have considerable manufacture carried on here and in several of the market towns round for weaving stockings by frames and one would scarce think it possible so small an article of trade could employ such multitude.

By the seventeenth century, the stocking frame was part of the working life of country stocking knitters too and people adapted their homes to accommodate the industry. Long windows would be added to existing workrooms or new rooms would be built to allow the plentiful light required for the craft.

By 1753, there were 1,000 frames in Shepshed alone. In 1801, out of a population of 1,628, 1,493 were involved in the hosiery trade. Stockingers worked long hours: approximately 70 per week, condensed into a five-day period.

By the nineteenth century, Leicestershire, Derbyshire and Nottinghamshire were the centre of the British hosiery industry. By 1832, Leicestershire was the dominant county, holding the majority of knitting frames.

The invention of the wide frame brought about another revolution, increasing productivity. But the new frames were too large for homes. Thus the mid nineteenth century marked the transition from home knitting to factory work.

The Luddites

But the advent of factory work was not well received by the knitters themselves. More efficient, large-scale production meant fewer workers were required.

Angry and afraid over the loss of their livelihoods, gangs of disgruntled workers began breaking into the new factories and destroying the machines. They became known as 'Luddites', after an Anstey man named Ned Ludd who lived in the late eighteenth century.

Ned was reputedly a simple boy and a target of local bullies. One day, while hiding from his tormentors in a knitter's cottage, Ned smashed a frame in anger. From then onwards, if something got broken, it was common to say that 'Ned Ludd's been at it again'.

Castle Street in Hinckley is the first known location of Luddite action, when angry workers who had been replaced by machinery took sledgehammers to the looms.

Naturally this threw the establishment into a panic. With the French Revolution still fresh in their minds, harsh penalties were put in place to attempt to curb this industrial sabotage, political dissent and social unrest. To restrict it, machine breaking was declared a capital crime.

But the Luddites continued undeterred, warning factory owners of their intent to destroy with letters signed 'Ned Ludd'.

In 1816, one particular group was apprehended for their machine breaking in the Loughborough factory of a Mr Heathcote – a night's work that ultimately cost them their lives.

First to be captured was James Towles, a stocking knitter. James was hung, but alone, as he staunchly refused to name his accomplices.

In January 1817, James Blackburn, another stockinger, was caught poaching. Blackburn injured the gamekeeper who caught him and needed to bargain for his life. So, to literally save his own neck, he turned King's evidence, admitted he had been part of the Loughborough raid and named his thirteen accomplices.

On 17 April 1817, six of those men – William Withers, Thomas Savage, John Amos, Jos Mitchell, John Crowther and Rodney Towles, James's younger brother, were hung at noon at Leicester Prison. A sympathetic crowd of 15,000 gathered to watch them die, singing hymns with them as they walked to the gallows as a show of solidarity.

Corah & Sons

Hosiery factories had existed in Leicestershire since the eighteenth century. Donisthorpe Mill in Leicester is one of the oldest mills in the east Midlands, manufacturing since the 1730s.

The most famous Leicestershire hosiery firm, was Corah's. Over its 150-year lifespan, the company employed thousands of Leicester people at its St Margaret's works, with other branches countrywide, supplying companies such as Marks & Spencer.

The company also had a reputation for benevolence towards its employees – especially in the early twentieth century. Older workers were retained until they wished to retire and the company encouraged sports, having its own bowling, skittles, cricket and football teams, as well inviting employees to an annual dinner.

Outside Leicester, Anstey, Earl Shilton and Kegworth were all key hosiery towns. Kegworth's stocking makers were so skilful that they supplied British and foreign royalty. Melton Mowbray also became famous for its 'Melton Cloth', a tightly woven, dense-piled woollen material first recorded in 1823. It was used to make sailors' coats and donkey jackets and, in North America, loggers' jackets.

But it was not only wool that was worked in Leicestershire. In 1809, the 'Twisted Lace Machine' found its way to Loughborough. The machine allowed for fine, lace-like work to be mass produced. So famous did the town become for its mittens that the machine was often referred to as 'the Loughborough machine'.

The Shoe Industry

Leather, as a by-product of cattle farming, was readily available In Leicestershire. But that wasn't the reason that Leicestershire became a major shoe manufacturer. In 1853, a Leicester shoemaker called Thomas Crick received the letters patent for his invention that would revolutionise the manufacture of boots and shoes. Crick had invented a riveting machine that fastened the uppers and soles of footwear together using 'tacks, rivets or sprigs' instead of stitches.

Crick's innovation allowed the shoe industry to become the second biggest Industry in Leicestershire. His invention increased the productivity and profitability of shoe making. In 1831, there were 425 boot and shoe manufacturers in the city of Leicester. By 1861, there were 2,741.

Shoemaking spread about the county. By 1863, Anstey had its first registered 'boot and shoe manufacturer' supplied by the village's leather industry. Earl Shilton was also a major shoe producer and established large factories such as Ortons, Eatoughs and Pinchess's. Leicester itself saw the establishment of firms such as Freeman, Hardy and Willis, and Oliver's.

Coal Mining

Coal had always been mined in Leicestershire, particularly in the 10-mile-square area in the north-west around Coleorton and Swannington.

In the Middle Ages, there were small pits around Swannington, Worthington, Staunton Harold and Swadlingcote. In the fifteenth century, Leicester Abbey also held an interest in mines at Oakthorpe.

The coal in these areas was generally on the surface. In 1572, it is recorded that gangs of fifteen to twenty men from Swannington were paid a shilling for every 1-2 tons of coal they gathered.

Where there were mines, they were not deep. At Coleorton, evidence from the late fifteenth century shows shafts only extended 30m below the surface.

The rich seams of coal lay deeper and thus out of reach until the Industrial Revolution. Then, in 1824, a mining engineer called William Stenson decided to try and sink a shaft on farmland near Whitwick. He struck lucky and found coal.

Mining exploded in the north-west of the county. By 1880, there were twenty-six pits centred around Whitwick, Bardon Hill, Ashby de la Zouch, Burton, Woodville, Netherseal, Ibstock, Bagworth, Swadlincote, Ibstock Coleorton, Snibson and Coalville.

But by the late twentieth century, mining began to die in Leicestershire. Thorn Tree drift, reservoir and Netherseal near Swadlingcote closed in the late 1940s. In the 1950s Donisthorpe, Calcutta, Oakthorpe and Ibstock collieries closed. The 1960s saw the closure of a further eight collieries. By the end of the late 1980s just one pit remained, Bagworth Colliery, which only survived until 1991.

In 1990, coalmining in Leicestershire underwent a brief renaissance with the Ashfordly super pit in the Vale of Belvoir. But in 1997 it too closed down due to 'unsurmountable geological problems'.

The Whitwick Colliery Disaster
Mining was fraught with dangers and accidents were common. In Leicestershire alone, 355 men are recorded as losing their

lives in the county's pits. So it is no surprise that miners were a superstitious bunch. The cry of the golden plover in particular warned of calamity in the pits.

The worst mining disaster in Leicestershire history occurred in 1898 at Whitwick Colliery. Forty-two men went down number five shaft that night. Only seven men returned alive.

The disaster was sparked by a gob fire, an underground blaze of disused material that became out of control. The flames consumed the wooden support timbers of the shaft roof, bringing about its collapse and raining fire on the miners trapped within.

As news of the disaster spread, crowds gathered to hope for the best – yet fearing the worst. Witnesses described how women sobbed 'as though their hearts were going to break'. A reporter from the *Mercury* was told by one of the rescue workers, 'They're all dead, my lad. I have worked in the pit 70 years and I know.'

Of the thirty-five men killed, only nine bodies were returned to the surface. Those bodies that were found were discovered huddled together with their arms around each other's necks. Many men's features were unrecognisable and at the inquest in January 1899 they could only be identified by the personal possessions found in their pockets.

The first body brought to the surface was that of Charles Clamp, who had managed to scramble to safety but then doubled back to help his comrades. The disaster's youngest victim was John Albert Gee of Thringston. He was just 13 years old. When thick smoke was noticed coming from the shaft, he was sent down the pit by the mine's deputy to order the men out.

Planes, Trains, Cranes, Iron and Automobiles

Engineering was, and still is, another major Leicestershire employer. The Ashfordby Hill steel works, near Melton Mowbray, were established in 1881 and are still going strong.

Initially owned by the Holwell Iron Company, the steel works were originally built to smelt iron. Later, a foundry was added so that iron could also be cast.

But as pig iron from abroad became cheaper in the 1950s and '60s, the company began to decline as an iron smelting plant. So Ashfordby branched out into steel manufacturing. It is now responsible for producing most of the drain covers in the UK. In 1996, it was also assigned the task of melting down a large number of weapons handed in to Leicestershire police as part of an amnesty.

Loughborough's Herbert Morris Ltd was established in 1885. Based at the town's Empress Works, it was famous for its cranes and joists, which it exported across the globe to places as varied as New Jersey and Korea. Its largest ever construct (a crane) weighed 400 tons.

The firm closed in 2010 when its then owner, Finnish company Konecranes, moved operations to Scotland.

Trains, planes and automobiles have all been made in Leicestershire. Sports car maker Noble Automobiles established itself in Barwell and Triumph Motorcycles in Hinckley. The Falcon Works in Loughborough began making turbines for steam locomotives and trams in 1865, before branching out into airborne vehicles during the First World War. From then on, the company continued to make and mend planes, providing a major service in the Second World War. Today, Mallory Park and Bruntingthorpe Aerodrome continue this tradition, providing testing facilities for automotive and aerospace engineers.

Not all of Leicestershire's engineering ventures were a success. In the early nineteenth century, the earls of Moira, Ireland, built an industrial village named after them near Coalville on the banks of the Ashby de la Zouch Canal. The centre of the village's industry was a blast furnace erected in 1805. But the venture was not a success. Not only was the local ironstone of poor quality, but the furnace didn't work effectively. It was abandoned in 1815 but survived because it was so little used – which is why the Moira

Furnace is one of the few surviving furnaces of this era and the area now a Scheduled Ancient Monument.

CRAFTS

Bell-founding

Leicestershire's earliest bell-founder was Johannes de Stafford, who is believed to have had a foundry in Leicester in the late fourteenth century. De Stafford was famed for his high-quality bells, which were installed in local churches at Aylestone, Beeby, Great Glen, Little Dalby, Loddington, Ratby, Shenton and Thrussington. De Stafford's foundry also cast a large bell for York Minster in 1371.

In his day, de Stafford was probably only one of many bell-founders in England. Today, Leicestershire has one of the only two bell-founding businesses left in the country. Based in Loughborough, John Taylor & Co. were established in 1839. Their

first commission was the recasting of bells for a local church. But by 1881 they had moved on to bigger things: namely, 'Great Paul' in St Paul's Cathedral. The bell was their largest commission, and at 16 tons it is still the largest bell in England.

Today, Taylors is the world's largest functioning bell foundry and regularly casts new bells for churches – including York Minster.

Stained Glass

Norman and Underwood are the oldest independent family run business in Leicester. The company began life in 1825 as a general plumbers and glaziers, but after several years the firm began to specialise in glass. In 1866, the company received its first and largest commission: to glaze the roof of St Pancras Station.

Work on many major churches and historic buildings followed, including Salisbury Cathedral, Windsor Castle, Westminster Abbey, Chatsworth House and Hampton Court.

The company also restore historic windows. One of their major projects was the restoration of St Ethelburga's, the historic church in Bishopsgate ravaged by an IRA bomb in 1993.

Pottery

Measham has been an area of clay extraction since the Middle Ages. From the nineteenth century it has also been the home of the famous Measham Ware – a local pottery covered with a dark brown glaze and painted with white clay flowers and a motto, for example 'Home is Best' and 'Friendship'.

Measham Ware was particularly associated with canal boats, as passing hauliers could order their pots as they passed through the town and collect the finished items on the return journey. Teapots were the most popular form of Measham Ware with seasonal farm workers from Norfolk and Suffolk who worked at the maltings of Burton upon Trent. They took the pots home as gifts for friends and family.

TRANSPORT

The Railway

William Stenson was not only the father of coalmining in Leicestershire but arguably the godfather of the railway in the county. Stenson recognised the potential of the fledgling transport system to his burgeoning industry and quickly sought out partners.

Joining with local landowner John Ellis and Ellis's friend George Stephenson, the designer of Stephenson's Rocket, Stenson formed the Leicester and Swannington Railway. Stephenson's son Robert became the railway's chief engineer.

Sixteen miles of track were built in two stages, with the first section of the line running from Leicester to Bagworth opening in 1832. The remainder was completed by 1836. The tunnel built by Stephenson at Glenfield near the line's first station was, at 1 mile 36 yards long, for a time the world's longest railway tunnel. As well as being the first railway in Leicestershire, the Leicester to Swannington railway was only the fifth line in the UK to be authorised and built.

The Canal

But before the railway, it was the canal that initiated Leicester's industrial growth.

The Grand Union Canal came to Leicestershire in the late eighteenth century bringing, in the words of the *Leicester Guardian*, 'extensive advantages to town and country'. Coal was the principle reason for its construction as the canal connected Leicestershire with nearby Derbyshire coalfields.

Foxton Locks were part of this canal system and boasted a particularly ingenious innovation. The natural incline of the land at the locks slowed down the canal boats, so that it took an hour to pass through. This was annoyingly inefficient. So, between 1897 and 1900, an inclined plane was built to speed up the passage through Foxton's ten locks. Instead of passing through each lock, the barges were loaded into a cradle and lifted up the hillside, cutting the journey time to ten minutes.

WORKING PEOPLE

Life on the Land

Life for a farmworker in Leicestershire was no bucolic dream. Discipline was strict. Some could even say it represented a form of paid bondage because of the rules imposed on workers – and the penalties for breaking them.

Even into the early twentieth century it was customary to refer to the farmer as 'master'. This was more than just a title of deference, for labourers' employers literally had control of their lives for the tenure of their employment. This control even extended to their supposed free time.

In 1869, two young labourers were arrested and taken before Lutterworth magistrates. Their crime was to go out after work without asking their employer's permission. The labourers were ordered to apologise for their 'crime' and pay a fine of seven shillings each – or face fourteen days in prison!

Farmers and their labourers would sign a contract of employment upon their hiring. Before the 1867 Master and Servant Act, any labourer who broke this contract by leaving prematurely was liable to be imprisoned. On the other hand, an employer who let his hireling go before time was only fined.

So it is little wonder that the town was a lure, perhaps seen as offering a freer or more prosperous life.

The Poor Law

In times of boom, it was easy to get a job. But when work dried up, as it did at various times in early nineteenth-century Leicestershire, then workers would be laid off without pay – very much like the zero contract workers of today.

No work meant no money. And that left the unemployed only two choices if they could not find alternative work: the parish or the poorhouse.

Initially, if the parish deemed you to be 'worthy', you would be maintained in your own home by being allowed 'out relief': vouchers, food and the basic necessities of life. But if for any reason you were branded as part of the 'unworthy poor', your only choice was the workhouse.

With the formation of the union workhouses in 1836, the practice of 'out relief' began to be phased out and from 1837 the able-bodied poor were also required to enter the workhouse.

During the depression of 1841, 5,000 people in Leicester were claiming relief. During this time, on average 25 per cent of workhouse residents were skilled workers who through no fault of their own had been left without work.

Besides Leicester, there were workhouses at Ashby de la Zouch, Barrow on Soar, Billesdon, Blaby, Hinckley, Loughborough, Lutterworth, Market Bosworth, Market Harborough and Melton Mowbray.

Before they became the responsibility of the borough, workhouses were little more than glorified sweatshops, run by private contractors who used the inmates as cheap labour for their own businesses. In Leicester in 1720, at a workhouse in St Martin's parish, inmates were required to work twelve hours a day at spinning or stocking making, between 6 a.m. and 8 p.m. in the summer and 7 a.m. until 9 p.m. in the winter.

Even after the establishment of union workhouses, things were little better. At Hinckley, the workhouse was known as 'The Bastille' with some inmates chained, accidentally poisoned or declared lunatics.

But not every workhouse regime was harsh. In the early twentieth century, the governor of Mountsorrel workhouse assessed the talents and attributes of inmates, allocating them work suitable to their skill set.

Slum Life

Having a job didn't guarantee you a decent standard of living. Many of Leicestershire's factory workers called the slums home. These badly built, basic residences had been constructed as quickly and cheaply as possible in order to profit from the flood of factory workers to Leicestershire's towns in the 1800s.

Leicester city centre was riddled with them, with Charles Street and the area around what is now the ring road a warren of unsanitary homes for the working poor. Notorious areas included Palmerston Street, Carley Street, Baker Street and Wharf Street – the last area to be cleared.

Houses were based around a cobbled central yard. Unheated and without independent supplies of water, what facilities there were were shared. Communal toilets often overspilled – providing the perfect breeding ground for disease.

In 1871, at the peak of Leicester's prosperity when industrialisation had made it one of the richest cities in the world, it was estimated that one in four children died of diarrhoea before their first birthday. This placed infant mortality in Leicester's slums at twice the national average.

Some claimed that the unrelenting harshness of the slums drove its residents to depravity. In the 1920s, Councillor Grimsley, a member of the Leicester borough and a Methodist minister, claimed many slum women had taken to drinking methylated spirits laced with lemon juice, to blot out the misery of their existence, harming both unborn and living children with their negligence.

But many felt statements like this were a way of displacing some of the blame for the dangers of life in the slums. Union leader Mary Bell Richards maintained that despite the hardships of their daily life, slum women were decent and hardworking and determined to make the best of things for themselves and their children.

Slum clearance began after the First World War with the drive for 'homes fit for heroes'. At first modernisation was attempted but it soon became clear that it was better to clear away the slums altogether. In 1929, Leicester Corporation gave the green light to demolition and in 1930 the bulldozers moved in and the residents moved out as the first slums in Leicester were destroyed. The former residents of these slums, on Green and Sandacre Streets, were moved to smart new homes on the newly constructed Talby estate.

Other Leicestershire towns followed, with Hinckley beginning its slum clearance later in the decade. But it was not until the 1950s that Leicestershire was slum free.

Industrial Unrest

It is a mistake to think that Leicestershire people accepted the hardships of working life without complaint – even if they weren't directly affected. In 1842, the people of Leicester rose up against the guardians of the workhouses who were forcing those still living off the parish in their own homes to break stone and rioted.

Nor was this the only protest of those times…

Thomas Cooper and the Chartists

Thomas Cooper was a poet and leading member of the Chartist movement, an organisation that believed in universal suffrage and workers rights. Cooper was born in Leicester on 20 March 1805. By trade a shoemaker, he self-educated himself, becoming a teacher before moving into journalism when he was 23.

After cutting his journalistic teeth in London and Lincoln, in 1840 Cooper returned home and joined the staff of the *Leicestershire Mercury*. By this time he was a dedicated Chartist and set about making Leicester a Chartist stronghold.

While at the *Mercury*, he published his own Chartist journal *The Commonwealthman* and became a leading lecturer for the movement. He also helped organise strikes in Leicestershire that were part of the general wave of discontent, brought about by hunger and mass unemployment in the northern counties during the summer of 1842.

Cooper organised miners' strikes over low wages and rallied disgruntled hosiery workers, who were working only half a week but still paying their employers full rent for their frames. The workers took to the streets of Leicester with banners and flags, calling for others to join them. Local magistrates, alarmed by the swelling crowds, swore in special constables to be on standby.

On 19 August, hundreds of strikers were listening to speakers at Humberstone Gate when they were advised by the speakers to arm themselves and hurry to Loughborough to support protesters under attack from the authorities.

But the police pursued them and turned them off the road at Mowacre Hill just outside the city. Although the yeomanry charged at the strikers, there was no blood spilled during the 'battle', although it did have the effect of ending the strikes – on this occasion.

On 26 August 1842, Thomas Cooper was arrested at his home at Church Gate, Leicester, and put on trial in Stafford for his part in riots in the Staffordshire Potteries. He was sentenced to two years in prison and whilst inside wrote 'Purgatory of Suicides', a 944-stanza poem discussing the dawning of an age of freedom and equality.

And 1842 wasn't the only year of disputing hosiery workers:

- In 1787, Coltham and Whetstone tried to introduce a steam stocking-making machine in Leicester. Local workers were enraged at the threat to their livelihood and rioted for a week, storming the home of the owners and wrecking the machine.
- In 1824 and 1826 in Hinckley strikes by framework knitters were so disorderly that the army had to be called in to manage the strikers.
- In 1859, 130 hosiery workers at Messrs Homer and Everard of Earl Shilton withdrew their labour and called upon workers from Leicestershire, Derbyshire and Nottinghamshire to join them.

The General Strike

Mass unemployment after the First World War led to further industrial unrest in the 1920s. In 1921, the Leicester unemployed rioted around the clock tower in the city centre. Further dissent followed in 1926, when low wages and poor working conditions in the mining industry led to the General Strike.

Over 7,000 people from trade unions joined the strike – the majority being railway workers. In Dunston Bassett near Harborough, one of the village's special constables was called upon to guard the local railway tunnel from striking railwaymen, who were believed to be planning to damage the tunnel to prevent coal being transported by train. The constable, who knew many of the men, did not believe they would damage railway property and sympathised with their cause. So he refused. As a result, he was ordered to give up his badge and resign.

The 1984/5 Miners' Strike

In Leicestershire in the mid-1980s, there were 2,500 miners but only thirty withdrew their labour during the Miners' Strike. While their colleagues ignored the decision to strike by the

National Union of Mineworkers, 'The Dirty Thirty' stood true to the cause, despite the financial hardship and peer pressure. The leader was Malcolm Pinnegar, who was led by the belief that Leicestershire miners should support mining comrades around the country who were fighting for their jobs.

They were right: by the end of the 1980s, most of Leicestershire's pits were closed.

Industrial Redevelopment

Many of Leicestershire's old industries and industrial sites are now defunct and closed. However, they have morphed into a new way for Leicestershire residents to make a living. The following are just a couple of examples.

Snibston Discovery Park

Built on the old north-west Leicestershire coalfields, this once derelict industrial area was turned into a recreational area and museum of science and working life in 1992.

Abbey Pump Station

Opened in 1891, the Abbey Pumping Station was Leicester's state-of-the-art sewerage works. The building's elegant architecture, like many of its type, belied its function. So too did its decorative beam engines. The sewerage works closed in 1964, but the pump station lives on – now as a museum of technology. The beam engines also remain, in full working order – the only place in Britain that such examples can be seen.

CRIME AND PUNISHMENT

PRISONS

Lock-Ups

Most Leicestershire towns and villages had small buildings for holding petty criminals or those awaiting transfer to the county gaols. Known as 'blind' houses or lock-ups, they were little more than stone sheds. Examples remain at Barrow upon Soar, Breedon-on-the-Hill, Castle Donington, Packington and Worthington.

The Old County Goal

The county gaol was always situated in the principle town of Leicestershire, Leicester. The first gaol was built in 1309. Before its existence, Leicester criminals were transported to Warwick goal after conviction.

The county gaol underwent several incarnations on Leicester's Highcross Street. The final gaol built on the site was constructed

 in the early 1790s. This gaol's first inmate was its architect, George Moneypenny, who was committed there between 1792 and 1793 for debt!

The prison had a fearsome reputation, described by one convict as 'hell on earth'. In the mid nineteenth century, it ran a separatist regime where prisoners were kept in isolation to prevent them from 'polluting' their fellow prisoners further.

In 1828, the county gaol moved to the newly constructed prison on Welford Road. The gaol on Highcross Street was now downgraded to the borough gaol, which it remained until its demolition in 1897.

Welford Road Prison

The prison was built in 1825 because of the inadequacy of the old county gaol. It covered 3 acres and was built to conform to new standards, designed to ensure that 'the security and comfort of the prisoners are specially regarded'.

The exterior was shaped like a medieval castle – which even today causes many unwitting tourists to queue outside in the mistaken belief it is Leicester Castle.

Executions took place on a temporary drop that was erected in front of the turreted entrance. The first hangings at the newly built Welford Road Prison took place on 20 April 1829, when three men were hanged for horse stealing.

Leicester's Bridewell Prisons

A bridewell was a sixteenth-century prison for petty criminals, based on the pattern of the original bridewell in London.

Leicester rather confusingly had two bridewells. The first, which stood near the old county goal on Highcross Street, was known by the nineteenth century as the House of Correction. The County Bridewell, on the other hand, was built not long before the new Welford Road Prison. This stood at the lower end of Oxford Street, near to Leicester Royal Infirmary. It was equipped for hard labour, with prisoners working treadmills to grind corn, some of which was used within the gaol and the rest sold to the public.

Prison Breaks

Perhaps the most daring prison break in Leicestershire's history was that of highwayman William 'swift Nick' Nevison.

Born to a respectable family in Pomfret in 1639, young Nevison was a bit of a lad – until he stepped over the line into crime, stealing money and a horse to make a new life in London.

After a stint in the army, Nevison began his career on the road, adopting the façade of a gentleman highwayman. He was chivalrous to women and kind to the poor and seems to have returned to the straight and narrow when he went home to make up with his father – only to return to his old ways on the old man's death.

It was during this time that he was caught in Leicestershire and committed to Leicester Gaol. Due to his notoriety, Nick was well secured and closely guarded. Escape looked unlikely. But he had a plan.

Firstly, he feigned illness and summoned a group of trusted friends, one of whom was a 'doctor'. This gentleman explained to the gaoler that Nick had a 'pestilential fever' and needed fresh air or the whole goal would be infected. Nick was duly unfettered and given his own room, and a nurse and doctor visited him twice a day – while the fearful gaolers gave him a wide berth!

This was just as Nick had planned. While unattended, the doctor painted Nick with blue plague spots and the fake patient was then dosed up to appear lifeless. One sight of the spots was enough for the gaoler, who was more than happy to see the infectious corpse out of his prison.

So swift Nick escaped Leicester Gaol in a coffin and for a while everyone did indeed believe he was dead – until his 'ghost' began once again 'haunting' the roads of Leicestershire, after which it slowly dawned on the authorities that swift Nick wasn't quite so dead after all.

Escape from the Old Borough Gaol

In 1867, 25-year-old John McCarty was serving seven years for jewel robbery in the borough gaol on Highcross Street. The prison was undergoing modification at the time, necessitating the demolition of part of the boundary wall.

One day, while exercising under guard, McCarty took his chance, dodging the warders and escaping through the gap in the wall. Dropping down into the street below, he was quickly away; the guards within the prison, unable to leave their prisoners for fear of other escapes through the prison's breached defences, could only blow their whistles to sound the alarm.

McCarty managed to make it as far as Fleckney Canal before the police caught up with him. But he didn't give up, trying to escape once again on the way back to Leicester, where he was finally safely locked up.

Welford Road Prison's Only Escapee

On 18 December 1953, renowned safe blower Albert Hattersley became Welford Road's only known escapee. Absconding through a skylight in the prison workshop, Hattersley scaled the prison wall and then made the drop into the governor's garden – and freedom!

Hattersley had hoped the soft ground would break his fall. He was wrong and he broke his ankle so badly part of the bone was left sticking out. But he still managed to get away from the prison – until the following day when he was recaptured. Who knows, maybe with a sound ankle, he could have made his escape?

Gartree Prison

The name of Gartree or Gove Tree commemorated an oak tree that marked an ancient meeting place for the elders of the Gartree hundred. Here, they held a court between 1458 and 1750. The open air apparently ensured the proceedings were free from the influence of the malign spirits of buildings!

The grove is now gone and in its place stands Gartree Prison. Opened in 1965, it has played host to such infamous inmates as Charles Bronson, Reggie Kray and Fred West.

In December 1987, the prison was the site of a dramatic and unique breakout. Lifer Sidney Draper and gang boss John Kendall, who was serving eight years, were lifted out of the prison yard in spectacular fashion by a stolen helicopter. Kendall was recaptured after ten days but murderer Draper remained at large for another thirteen months.

THE ASSIZES

The assizes were periodic courts held around English counties until 1972, when they were replaced with the county court system. They dealt with the most serious crimes.

The great hall of Leicester Castle was used for Leicestershire's assizes from 1273 until 1888, when it became the location of the county court until its closure in 1990.

Its 800 years of use makes it one of the longest-running courtrooms in England – beaten only by Oakham Castle, which was in use from 1229 and is still occasionally used today.

PUNISHMENTS

Hanging Places in Leicestershire
The major execution sites in Leicestershire were:

The Dane Hill Tollgate on Hinckley Road, Leicester; **Red Hill**, near Belgrave; **Infirmary Square**, near to Leicester Prison was overlooked by Leicester Infirmary, from which patients were allowed to watch the hangings; **Gallowtree Gate**, which today can be found at the bottom of London Road at the heart of Leicester's city centre. The name originates further out of town, to the south, at the junction of what is now London Road and Evington Road after the place where gallows were erected.

Alternative Punishments
The cucking stool seems to have been a Leicestershire favourite for dealing with intransigent women. The stool was in fact a chair, in which the unfortunate woman was confined. Therein, she was conveyed through the streets until her journey's end – which was often a wet one! In Loughborough, the favourite culmination to a journey in the cucking stool was a dunking in the river, near to Cotes Mill.

Assizes records from Leicester in June 1654 detail the sort of incidents that merited such public humiliation. A Thomas Goadby laid a complaint against Ann Rawlins, a Leicester widow who apparently harangued both him and a Mrs Clarke in the street.

Mrs Rawlins cast aspersions of the worst kind – and in the ripest language – upon the character of Mrs Clarke's husband. She was found guilty and sentenced to the cucking stool.

It seems a great many people took to insulting Mrs Clarke, because at the same assizes she accused yet another woman of verbally abusing her – this time the wife of one Richard Pole. But the assizes seemed to think nothing of this strange coincidence, sentencing the unfortunate Mrs Pole to the same humiliating punishment.

LOCAL LAWMEN

Frederick Goodyer

Leicester Police Force was established in 1836 under Frederick Goodyer, one of the very first police officers in Sir Robert Peel's new Metropolitan Police Force. After three years heading Leicester Borough Police, Goodyer became the chief constable of the newly formed Leicestershire County Police Force.

Francis 'Tanky' Smith

Francis 'Tanky' Smith was a celebrated detective inspector with Leicester police for twenty-four years. He and his partner Tommy 'black tommy' Haines joined up in 1840 as the fledgling force's first detectives. Wearing disguises, the pair infiltrated local criminal gangs to collect evidence for convictions. Their high arrest records made them the town's most successful officers.

In 1862, Tanky dealt with his most famous case, the Winstanley Affair. Local squire and High Sheriff of Leicestershire Mr James Beaumont Winstanley had mysteriously disappeared and Tanky was tasked with tracking him down. The trail took the detective to the Continent and ended in Germany where the High Sheriff was found drowned.

Tanky spent his £1,000 reward from the case on a row of houses on London Road. Designed by his architect son, the terrace became known as Top Hat Terrace from the carvings of Tanky wearing his police top hat – and the variety of disguises he adopted in his work.

In 1863, citing 'failing eyesight and bodily strength', Tanky retired from the force. Retirement, however brief, obviously had restorative powers, for almost immediately he set himself up as Leicester's first private detective.

The Laughing Policeman

PC John William 'Tubby' Stevens was equally as famous as 'Tanky' Smith – but for different reasons. He was a popular and well-loved Leicester bobby who served for twenty-two years – despite his considerable girth. At his death in 1908 at only 48, Tubby weighed 23 stone 3lb and was believed to be England's heaviest policeman.

An estimated 10,000 people turned out to pay their respects on the day of his funeral, lining the route from his house to Welford Road cemetery.

Tubby is said to be the inspiration behind the song 'The Laughing Policeman' because of his jolly, good-humoured nature.

John Marriot

In 1962, local tailor John Marriot began his service as a Leicestershire special constable, patrolling the Belgrave and Beaumont Leas areas.

In 1982, he was awarded a long service medal, having served for twenty years. But his work with Leicestershire police did not end there. After a stint as a truancy officer, in 2000 John returned to Leicestershire police as a police support volunteer, monitoring CCTV footage from around Leicestershire at Melton police station every Wednesday morning. John was still going strong at 85!

EARLY GANGS

The De Folvilles

John de Folville, Lord of Ashby, had seven sons. After his death in 1310, his eldest son John took over the estate. But his other six sons formed a notorious medieval gang that terrorised Leicestershire throughout the 1320s and 1330s.

The gang's first crime is recorded by Henry of Knighton. On 29 January 1326, a Master Roger Bellers was found murdered near Rearsby. His death was laid squarely at the door of 'one Eustace de Folville and his brothers'.

Bellers was a greedy fellow, apparently guilty of persecuting and threatening the de Folvilles, as well as many of his other neighbours. So this initial murder may have been tolerated if not secretly well received by locals. However, the de Folvilles were still outlawed.

This changed in 1329 when they were pardoned by the king on the condition that they fought for him. This period of reconciliation with authority did not last. While in the garrison at Leicester, the gang robbed the town burgesses. In 1330, the pardon was revoked.

The de Folvilles quickly became a public nuisance, committing more murders and robberies. By 1331, they were at risk of further censure by the law. To forestall this, Richard de Folville, 'a wild and daring man and prone to acts of violence', who was also the rector of Teigh, kidnapped the king's justice Richard de Willoughby as he travelled to Grantham.

Willoughby was only released after he paid his kidnappers 90 marks and swore an oath to 'comply with their instructions' – which was presumably to protect them from outlawry.

Eustace de Folville, the eldest of the gang, managed to elude justice, dying a natural death in 1347 having served the king in the Hundred Years War. However, Richard did not fare so well. In 1340, justice finally caught up with him as the ruthless rector sought sanctuary in his own church with two other gang members. A stand-off between the criminals and their pursuers occurred with the Reverend de Folville killing one man with his bow before he was eventually dragged from the church and beheaded.

Because he was a priest, Richard's death was deemed unlawful, so his killers had to do penance by praying for forgiveness outside all the neighbouring churches before being publicly beaten with a rod!

The Ash Tree Operatives

Seventeenth-century Leicestershire was an equally lawless place. With no established police force, local constables were often unwilling to take action against criminals in remote areas.

Eaton in particular was a popular haunt for local criminals and murder, violence and looting was commonplace. So to answer the problem, a group of ten local men became vigilantes. Establishing their hideout in the Eaton countryside, they became known as the 'Ash Tree Operatives', after the entrance to their hideout, which was through a hollowed-out ash tree.

NOTORIOUS CRIMES AND CRIMINALS

George Davenport

Born in 1758 in Wigston, George Davenport was Leicestershire's most famous highwayman.

George was apprenticed to a framework knitter, but he had no appetite for work, preferring to drink with his rowdy friends. George turned to crime for money when he left his apprenticeship, cutting his teeth on fraud. His favourite practice was to find an army recruitment sergeant, join up and pocket the advance money always paid to new recruits. After a session in the inn at the sergeant's expense, George would leave the unconscious recruiting officer and do a runner, often on a stolen horse. By his own account, George deserted from no less than forty regiments in this way.

George did eventually join up, serving as a British solider during the American War of Independence, but after his army career folded, he returned home and took to the Leicestershire highways as a robber.

For eighteen years he plied his trade and became mythologized as some sort of a Robin Hood figure who robbed the rich and gave to the poor of Oadby and Wigston.

One evening, he was drinking in the Bull's Head in Belgrave when he saw a poster offering a reward for his capture. 'I am George Davenport, catch me if you can,' he goaded the drinkers, before hightailing it off the premises, leaving behind his dumbfounded would-be capturers.

But in August 1797, George's luck ran out. A butcher he was attempting to rob bested him and handed him over to the constable. He was tried and convicted of highway robbery, and driven to hang at the Red Hill gallows. George, however, had the last laugh. It was customary for the hangman to claim everything belonging to an executed criminal 'outside the shroud'. George, wily to the end, went to his death with his shroud over his clothes – effectively cheating the hangman of his bounty.

George's son, William, also joined the army, serving as a sergeant in the Royal Marines. After leaving, he too ended up in the county goal – but as head turnkey, rather than a prisoner.

Earl Ferrers

Laurence Shirley, the 4th Earl Ferrers, owned estates in Derbyshire and Northamptonshire but his main residence was at Staunton Harold Hall, close to Ashby de la Zouch.

Ferrers was a womanizer and a drinker. He destroyed his marriage with his violent and erratic behaviour towards his wife, which was so bad she was granted a separation by Act of Parliament in 1758. As part of the separation, Ferrers was forced to make a financial settlement on his wife, a fact he bitterly resented. It fell to his old family steward, John Johnson, to administer this allowance. Ferrers discovered Johnson was also secretly bestowing Lady Ferrers with extra income without him knowing, which deepened his antipathy towards his servant.

On Sunday, 18 January, Ferrers invited Johnson to visit the hall to discuss business. His live-in mistress and their children, plus the other servants, were sent away, leaving the pair alone. At around 3 p.m., Ferrers and Johnson had a heated argument and Ferrers shot his steward. The wound was not fatal and Ferrers called a Dr Kirkland to attend to Johnson, but while the medic was treating his patient the earl continued to drunkenly abuse his victim before falling into a stupor. Before doing so, according to Kirkland he made the following admission: '… that he had intended to shoot him [Johnson] dead, for that he was a villain, and deserved to die; "but," said he, "now that I have spared his life, I desire you would do what you can for him".'

Johnson died the following day and Dr Kirkland enlisted the support of a number of local men to disarm and arrest the earl. The inquest brought in a verdict of wilful death and so Ferrers was remanded to Leicester Prison. As he was a peer of the realm, the Leicester Assizes did not have jurisdiction over him, so he was transferred to the Tower of London on 14 February and committed to the custody of Black Rod.

On 16 April 1760, in Westminster Hall, Ferrers pleaded insanity – which was not unfeasible as everyone who knew him thought him mad. But after conducting his defence 'clearly and cognently', his fellow peers rejected his plea and as the evidence left them no other choice, Ferrers was found guilty and sentenced to death. He was the last peer of the realm in Britain to suffer that fate.

Having been denied beheading – the usual mode of execution for a peer – on 5 May 1760 the earl found himself on his way to the death of a common criminal at Tyburn.

A special new gallows complete with black baize had been constructed for the occasion. The earl travelled in his own carriage, in his wedding suit, for 'he thought this at least as good an occasion for putting them on as that for which they were first made.' He died at around noon, having showed more style and courage at his death than on many occasions in life. His body was buried at St Pancreas church after dissection, but twenty-two years later taken back to Staunton Harold and the family crypt.

Topsy-Turvy

John Massey of Bilstone was a farm labourer and famous local wrestler. He became known as Topsy-Turvy for defeating his opponents by throwing them over his head.

Massey was also a known drunk with a violent temper. He was known to be cruel to his first wife, Sarah, who died in 1797. However, this did not deter a second woman from marrying him, despite the fact she had a young daughter. The union was not a happy one and its end tragic. One evening in 1800, the family were walking near Bilstone Mill. Massey and his wife had a violent argument that culminated in the wrestler losing his temper and brutally beating his wife before kicking her and her daughter into the millstream. Mrs Massey died, but her daughter survived, leaving her as the prime witness. Massey was tried at Leicester Assizes and found guilty. He was sentenced to hang and be gibbetted after his death. On 23 March 1801, he was executed at Red Hill in Birstall and a day later his body was transported for gibbeting in the parish where the crime was committed. The body was wrapped in chain and hung from a metal ring on the gibbet post as a gruesome spectacle for passers-by. As late as 1818, the remains of Topsy-Turvy reputedly remained in place.

John Cook

In 1832, John Cook was a 21-year-old Leicester bookbinder with his own workshop on Wellington Street. But Cook was in trouble – money trouble.

Cook owed money to a London engraver called John Paas. On a fateful visit to Leicester, in May 1832, Paas visited Cook at his workshop to demand payment. An argument ensued and Cook hit Paas on the head, killing him.

In a panic, Cook dismembered the body, and, drinking heavily to steady his nerves, began to try and dispose of the remains in his workshop fire. But Cook's fireplace was not built for such a grisly task. The fire was soon out of control and the neighbours alerted the authorities, who arrived to investigate. An inebriated Cook explained he was disposing of a rotten piece of dog meat. But his visitors were not convinced and took the 'meat' away. On examination, it proved to be the pelvis and thigh of a human.

Paas's absence and the fact his pencil case was found at the scene helped identify him as the victim. Cook, in the meantime, had attempted to flee to America – only to be apprehended as his boat was about to leave Liverpool docks.

He was found guilty at Leicester and sentenced to hang and be gibbetted – making him the last man in England whose remains suffered that fate.

Peppermint Billy

Born near Scalford, William 'Peppermint Billy' Brown gained his nickname from his father's occupation as a mint maker.

Billy did not follow in his father's footsteps. In 1843 he was sentenced to ten years' transportation after stealing a horse at Newton Linford. He served his sentence in Tasmania and in 1856 returned to England.

But it was not long before Billy was once again in trouble with the law. On 20 June 1856, the bodies of toll keeper Edward Woodcock and his 10-year-old grandson were found in the Thorpe Arnold gatehouse. Seventy-year-old Mr Woodcock had been stabbed many times and shot. His grandson's throat was cut.

Billy was implicated because he had had an altercation with the elderly toll keeper two days earlier when the old man refused him a drink of water. Perhaps more damning were certain items that could be associated with him found at the scene. A tobacco stopper and pistol of the type used by Australian bushrangers were found close to the bodies, and a bloodstained shirt was discovered dumped nearby.

A £20 reward was offered for Billy's capture and his description was circulated around the country. He was eventually arrested in Yorkshire and returned to Melton Mowbray to await trial.

Billy's protests of innocence came to nothing and he was convicted. His was the last public hanging in Leicestershire on 25 July 1856, in front of a crowd of 25,000 who gathered outside Welford Road Prison. Billy made no speech but was calm and collected as he went to his death. His father, who witnessed his execution, certainly approved, as he was heard to say, 'Well done, Billy. Thas died a brick.'

A Controversial Acquittal

On Saturday, 5 July 1919, the body of 21-year-old Annie Bella Wright was found lying next to her bicycle on Stretton Lane, Little Stretton. Initially, it was thought that Bella had died in a freak fall. But careful examination of the scene by officer PC Hall revealed a .455 bullet was trodden into the road surface near the body. Further investigation revealed Bella had been shot just below her left eye.

It seemed that a mysterious man on a green bicycle was key to events. He had been observed watching and following Bella on her fateful trip to Stretton. Eventually, a green bicycle was fished out of Leicester Canal. It was identified as belonging to Roland Light, an ex-army officer and schoolteacher. Light had been issued with a .455 revolver while in the army.

On his arrest, Light admitted he had dumped the bike for fear that it incriminated him. He also admitted to being with Bella on the day of her death, but denied the killing.

Light was tried at Leicester Castle Assizes and defended by one of the best advocates of the age, Sir Edward Marshall Hall. Despite the evidence, Light was acquitted, but many Leicester people believed he was guilty of the murder.

NOT SO NOTORIOUS CRIMES

The Murder of Thomas Barrett

The 30 November 1886 was an ordinary day for the residents of Breedon-on-the Hill until James Banton, a local poacher, appeared running drunkenly down the High Street, waving a stick and announcing, 'I just killed a bobby!'

The 'bobby' was Thomas Barrett, one of a group of officers who had arrested Banton and a friend for poaching six months earlier. Banton and an associate had come across PC Barrett and decided to pick a fight with the policeman. But the fight ended with PC Barrett being beaten to death with his own baton.

Banton's friend had left the scene before the attack began, which led to his acquittal, but for Banton his drunken altercation led to the noose.

PC William Wilkinson

PC Wilkinson was well liked in Sileby. A 'nice fellow who would rather see a man home than lock him up' was how locals remembered him. He was well thought of in the Leicestershire force too, earning himself a merit stripe for good conduct.

On 25 May 1903, just before leaving for his nightshift patrolling the streets of Sileby, PC Wilkinson's little girl cried, 'Daddy I don't want you to go out again tonight.' PC Wilkinson reassured her he would be home soon and left.

But he never came home. At around 11 p.m., Wilkinson investigated a rustling in the bushes around St Mary's churchyard. Suddenly, two figures sprang up from behind a gravestone, firing at Wilkinson, who reeled down the road a few paces before falling down dead.

Local shoe hands Thomas Preston and Thomas Porter were arrested for the crime. They were known to bear a grudge against Wilkinson and his fellow officer PC Hall, who had arrested them previously for poaching and disorderly drinking, Preston threatening to 'shoot the pair of you'.

On the day in question, both had been drinking heavily since midday and half an hour before the murder, Porter was heard to tell a friend, 'You may hear something in the morning.'

Officers went to Porter's house where the two were holed up. The pair, still clearly drunk and brandishing a shotgun, refused to surrender. A siege began which lasted until the next morning, by which time they had sobered sufficiently to see some sense and end their resistance. They were found guilty and hanged at Leicester Prison, despite pleading their innocence until the end.

A Question of Time

William Palmer was an itinerant fish seller. In January 1911, he made the journey to Lutterworth from Folkstone to sell his wares.

The day after he left the district for home, a local widow, Mrs Harris, was found strangled in her home. Scattered around her were her savings. Questions were asked and Palmer fell under suspicion because he paid for his train fare home with a handful of silver coins – when the day before he had been penniless.

On 25 January 1911, Palmer was arrested for Mrs Harris's murder. He denied the charges, claiming he had found the money, and although there was no other evidence against him, he was held in custody for five months on various pretexts.

At the end of this period, the landlord of the Rugby Hotel where Palmer broke his journey home, decided to clean out the toilet cisterns – and found a watch, gold chain and purse identified as belonging to Mrs Harris.

Palmer was tried at Leicester Assizes for murder. One expert witness claimed the watch had only been in the cistern for a few days, while another believed it had been there for just a couple of months. Either way, this meant that it could not have been placed there by Palmer. But when pressed, the second expert agreed the few months could actually have been five. This was sufficient to convict him.

'I am as innocent as a newborn babe,' Palmer declared as sentence was passed.

Palmer may well have been innocent of Mrs Harris's murder. But he had served time for murder in South Africa as a teenager and was wanted for a murder in Manchester. He fought all the way to the gallows on the day of his execution, yelling at officials, 'Are you going to let these fellows murder me?'

The Amorous Highwayman

Jack Ovet was born in Nottingham and was a shoemaker by trade. But like so many who took to a life of crime in the eighteenth century, he wanted more from life. Jack liked to drink and aspired to be a gentleman so he took to the road as a highwayman.

Ovet did reasonably well from his new career, and developed a reputation for a certain gallantry. On one occasion, one of his victims claimed Ovet had only bested him because he took him by surprise. Ovet graciously returned the £20 he had taken from the man and challenged him to make good his claim in a one to one fight with swords. Ovet won – and reclaimed the stolen £20.

But events took a more romantic turn when Ovet robbed the Worcester stagecoach. Several young women handed over their valuables to the highwayman that day. But one of them stole his heart. As he robbed her, Ovet reputedly said:

Madam, cast not your eyes down, neither cover your face with those modest blushes; your charms have softened my temper, and I am no more the man I was. What I have taken from you (through mere necessity at present) is only borrowed; for as no object on earth ever had such an effect on me as you, assure yourself that if you please to tell me where I may direct to you, I'll upon honour make good your loss to the very utmost.

Somewhat surprisingly, the lady gave the highwayman her address and in a week she received a letter from him – not to return her money but to propose!

Madam,

These few lines are to acquaint you that though I lately had the cruelty to rob you of twenty guineas, yet you committed a greater robbery at the same time in robbing me of my heart; on which you may behold yourself enthroned, and all my faculties paying their homage to your unparalleled beauty. Therefore be pleased to propose but the method how I may win your belief. ... For by all my hopes, by all those rites that crown a happy union, by the rosy tincture of your checks, and by your all-subduing eyes, I prize you above all the world ... Let us taste the pleasures which Cupid commands, and for that unmerited favour I shall become another man, to make you happy. So requesting the small boon of a favourable answer to be sent me to Mr Walker's, who keeps an ale-house at the sign of the Bell in Thornbury, in Gloucestershire, give me leave to subscribe myself your most humble servant to command for ever.

The lady, however, was not seduced – and more than a little annoyed that her money had not been returned:

You have already broken your word in not sending what you villainously took from me, but not valuing that, let me tell you, for fear you should have too great a conceit of yourself, that you are the first, to my remembrance, whom I ever hated; and sealing my hatred with the hopes of quickly reading your dying speech, in case you die in London, I presume to subscribe myself yours never to command.

Finding himself unlucky in love, the rest of Jack's luck quickly ran out. After a botched robbery in Leicestershire, he was pursued, caught and condemned to hang on 5 May 1708. But for his amorous interlude, his career would have been totally unremarkable.

Murderous Miners

In 1877, three Coalville miners were found guilty of murdering a peddler. On the scaffold, one of them confessed that the other two were innocent and he alone was responsible for the crime: the authorities still hanged all three.

Motoring Offences

With the advent of the twentieth century, motoring offences began to become a category of crime in themselves. The year 1899 saw the first speeding prosecution in Leicestershire when a motorist was caught on Taylor's Hill in Glenfield travelling in excess of 18mph! He was fined 15 shillings.

That was only the beginning. From 1923, Leicester city police used an unmarked motorbike, a Triumph SD, to catch speeding motorists. The model had just come second in the Isle of Man TT and held a number of speed records at the time. PC Thomas William Haywood chose and was assigned the bike. Dressed like a gamekeeper, the young PC patrolled the roads and reported two drivers on his first day and four on his second. Their penalty was a 40 shilling fine and the loss of their license for six months.

Hannah Read

When Hannah Read's husband deserted her and their five children to flee from his creditors, it was perhaps understandable that she took up with a man called Waterfield and had his child. James Read was gone for two years, but when he returned home in 1825, he demanded Hannah return to him at the marital home in Foxton. Hannah agreed, but on the day of her return she suddenly sent for her brother-in-law. She told him that on the journey home, James had 'run away from her mad and had jumped into the water [at Foxton Lock] and drowned himself.'

Hannah's brother-in-law did not believe her and the next day she was arrested. Her husband's body was recovered from the lock and witnesses also came forward at her trial: they claimed that Hannah had threatened to 'do for' James. After only fifteen minutes of deliberation, the jury found her guilty of James's murder.

Hannah's pleas for clemency as a mother failed and with death finally inevitable, she confessed. She said she distracted James by asking him for some money and as he reached into his pocket, pushed him into the canal.

On the morning of her execution, 5 August 1825, Hannah was taken to the bridewell. Here, she was attached to a sledge rather than loaded into a cart. This additional punishment was because her crime was counted as petty treason because she had murdered her husband. In front of quite a considerable crowd she was dragged to her execution and after attending the chaplain, taken to the scaffold and hanged.

Her case was publicised in twenty papers around the country, to act as a warning to other wives who might wish to be rid of their husbands – no matter what the justification.

COMIC CRIMES

The Drunken Nun of Quorn

In December 1885, a Sister Mary Frances of the 'convent Quorndon' was taken before Loughborough Petty Sessions and charged with assaulting local manufacturer's wife Mrs W. Wright. Sister Mary had visited the Wright house on 16 December to ask for contributions to the relief of the local homeless. Mrs Wright declined – probably because the nun seemed somewhat the worse for wear. Sister Mary then asked for a donation of brandy for a poor woman one of the sisters was nursing. Mrs Wright – perhaps to get rid of her – said she'd send the brandy if Sister Mary would give her the address. Realising she was getting nowhere, the inebriated nun began to beat Mrs Wright between the shoulders until the lady's servants pushed her out the door. However, the stroppy Sister then forced her way in a second time and when she was finally securely evicted, began to shake the doors and windows.

Once she had sobered up, the repentant nun wrote to Mrs Wright, apologising for 'anything that had occurred'. Despite having no memory of events, she denied the assault but was found guilty and was ordered to pay 15 shillings or face seven days in prison.

Road Rage in Quorn

Road rage is clearly not a modern phenomenon. In 1896, William Richardson, a Quorn butcher, was accused of trying to run Charles Hodgkin off his bike. Hodgkin had the temerity to ring his bell and overtake Richardson's vehicle. In response, Richardson sped up and despite Mr Hodgkin slowing to allow him to pass, the butcher proceeded to zig-zag across the road to prevent the cycle from passing. Richardson was travelling so fast he nearly collided with another oncoming vehicle. This had the effect of stopping him and he allowed Mr Hodgkin to pass him again.

But Richardson sped after him and at Mountsorrel caught up, calling to him 'Stop! I will stop you!' Richardson then overtook him but Mr Hodgkin later found him in the road at Mountsorrel Hill, after finally colliding with another vehicle.

Once summoned, Richardson blamed cyclists for his speeding. But Richardson was the worse for drink according to the policeman at the scene and the bench agreed, convicting Richardson of drink driving and attempting to run a cyclist down. He was fined £2.

And the vehicle in which this reckless pursuit occurred? Nothing more than a horse and cart!

GHOSTLY GOINGS-ON

HAUNTED HOUSES

Belgrave Hall

Belgrave Hall was once a grand country house. Now Belgrave is a suburb of Leicester and the house a museum.

But it seems some of the house's former residents have not moved on. Odd smells of baking bread and gingerbread waft

through the rooms when no one is cooking, and hushed voices and mysterious footsteps have been heard about its corridors.

The hall's famous Grey or Green Lady is believed to be Charlotte Ellis, one of seven sisters who lived at the hall in the nineteenth century. Charlotte died there aged 81 in 1917, still a spinster. Her spirit reputedly roams the gardens. It was here on 23 December 1998 that CCTV apparently spotted her ghost when a misty white shape was captured on film. But this theory was debunked by a series of paranormal investigators who claimed instead it was a leaf falling in front of the camera.

But the Grey Lady may not be alone. Paranormal experts believe she shares the hall with a 'negative male energy' upstairs, as well as a child who died of tuberculosis and a male ghost who was killed in a fall.

Papillon Hall

Papillon Hall used to be a mile west of Lubenhall near Lutterworth before it was demolished in the 1950s. But the legend of its ghost – and maybe the restless spirit itself – still remain.

The hall was built in 1622 on the site of a holy well by the Papillon family. But its sinister reputation dates back to the time of the great-grandson of the original builder, David Papillon, or 'Pamps'.

Pamps was a handsome man with a sinister reputation. He was believed to have harmful hypnotic powers. He also reputedly kept a Spanish mistress imprisoned in the attic of the house.

This mistress is said to have died in 1715 although her burial was never recorded. Soon afterwards, Pamps married and left Papillon Hall and the area. But he left behind a portrait of himself and a pair of lady's dancing shoes, with strict instructions that neither should be removed from the hall.

All was well at the hall as long as the objects remained in place – as future occupants discovered to their cost. When the Bosworth family sold the hall, they bequeathed its contents to one of their daughters. The new owner, Lord Hopeton and his household were quickly plagued by unexplained knockings and misfortunes. Events culminated one terrifying night in 1866 when the entire household gathered in the lobby while they listened to the sounds of furniture being thrown violently around the empty drawing room. On investigation everything remained in its rightful place.

The shoes and portrait were traced and reinstated. But history repeated itself when the shoes were loaned to the Paris Exhibition. The family in residence at the time had to move out for the duration of the shoes' absence.

The shoes were then secured in the hall in a wall safe. But during alterations to the hall in 1903 they were removed again. A worker was subsequently killed by a falling brick, while the owner, Lord Bellville, was hurt in a pony and trap accident.

During the Second World War, the government requisitioned the house for American servicemen. A group of the soldiers decided to test out the curse. They soon came to regret their decision and quickly returned the shoes to the hall.

So who was the ghost – Pamps or his dead mistress? Pamps' portrait seems to have had an unsettling reputation, with many owners finding it evil. But the shoes seem to be the key, so perhaps it is the mysterious Spanish mistress who is the restless spirit. During the 1903 renovations, the skeleton of a woman was found encased in the walls. Could this explain why there is no record of her burial?

On the hall's demolition, the shoes were reclaimed by a Papillon descendant and gifted to the Leicester Museum and the grounds became a farm. But it seems that even though the house has gone, a presence remains. The Hughes family who own the farm have heard strange noises around the old stable blocks, which still survive, as well as an eerie feeling of a presence about the land.

Wigston College

Once upon a time, Wigston College was the site of one of the grandest houses in the area, Heatherley House. But although the house is gone, it seems its last owner remains.

In the 1980s, a cleaner at the college reported hearing a woman calling her name – despite there being no one there. The caretakers explained that it was the former owner of the old house, who caused no harm but did like to tap people on the shoulder and otherwise disrupt them. Some weeks later, the cleaner saw the ghost for the first time, crossing a path by the workshops and walking out through a wall, dressed in a long black dress with a bunch of keys at her waist.

The ghost is reputedly the second wife of the house's original owner. After her husband's death, the county council offered to buy the house and grounds to build a college but the lady refused and threatened to curse any establishment on her land. But when the old lady was finally taken into care, the guardians of the estate sold the house and grounds.

The house was demolished and the college constructed. On her death, it seems she returned to her old home to watch over it. Reputedly a good lady in life, she continues to be so in death as none of her manifestations have been sinister.

Other Haunted Houses

In 1778, a house in Earl Shilton was said to be plagued by its former long-dead occupant. Tables and chairs danced about the room, while pewter dishes jumped off the shelves. But the alarm caused by the poltergeist grew when wigs and hats flew off the heads of their wearers. Villagers agreed that the spirit was a local man who could not rest in his grave because he had been defrauded in life.

Once a grand house owned by the Winstanley family, Braunstone Hall in Leicester is reputedly haunted by Georgina Winstanley, who died when a novice nun. It seems she returned to her family home after her untimely death, as her ghost was seen by servants, members of the Winstanley family and by staff when the house became a school.

Now a conference centre, Bosworth Hall in Market Bosworth once had a perpetual wet bloodstain and is haunted by a Grey Lady, reputedly Ann Dixie who bled to death in the eighteenth century after being caught in a man trap set by her father to capture her gardener lover.

Bushby Old Hall, demolished in 1965, only yielded its ghosts as its walls came down. As demolition proceeded, perfectly sturdy parts of the building began falling down of their own accord; workers heard strange noises and events culminated in one terrified builder running away after an encounter with a spectral old lady. The ghost was identified as Mary, a former maid at the hall who took her own life. The disturbances – and the ghost – disappeared with the last of the rubble.

In 1906 at The Spring's House, Lutterworth, a maid woke suddenly to see a young man in old-fashioned clothing standing at the foot of her bed. He then vanished into thin air, so terrifying the girl that she refused to stay overnight in the house again. The phantom is believed to be John Cook, a resident of the house fifty years earlier who was murdered on the premises.

The first person to report a ghost at The Cedars (aka Thomas Moore's House), Kegworth, was the Irish poet Thomas Moore, who wrote to a friend complaining of it in 1812. The phantom is supposedly that of a murdered butler and at one time the bloodstain of the crime was impossible to wash away.

HAUNTED PUBS

The Talbot Inn
The Talbot Inn lies 3 miles from Leicester city centre. It was originally built in the 1600s and was the last stop for condemned felons on the way to the Red Hill Gallows at Birstall. Many of the condemned also returned to the inn after their visit to the gallows, as one of the inn's outbuildings was used to accommodate the medical dissections of the remains of those not claimed for burial.

Unsurprisingly, several mysterious figures have been seen drifting around the inn's gardens, believed to be the restless spirits of those unfortunate souls. But the inn is also haunted on the inside. Pool balls frequently knock together of their own accord, while drinkers experience the classic chilly spots. Here, the ghosts include a cheerful young boy, and a young woman brushing her dishevelled hair – believed to be the ghost of a woman who died in childbirth.

The Blue Boar Inn

Sadly demolished in the nineteenth century, Leicester's Blue Boar Inn was reputedly haunted by the ghost of one of its landladies, Agnes Clarke, who was murdered for her money in 1613. After the inn was demolished, a new pub of the same name was established on Southgate Street. Agnes's ghost duly followed.

Frederick Mason, a landlord of the inn in 1958, refused to believe in the ghost despite warnings from his regulars. When he fell down the cellar stairs and broke his ankle, he put it down to an unlucky accident. Even cracking a rib in a coughing fit brought on by a bad cold was put down to bad luck. But all disbelief was suspended when he woke one night to see a white figure moving towards his bed. Agnes's ghost, now satisfied that Mr Mason was now a believer, never visited him again.

Other Ghostly Pubs

Agnes Clarke is not the only publican unable to call time on her duties. The spirit of Alice Johnson, once landlady of the Royal Oak at Great Dalby, also can't let go of her former occupation. Her fiery spirit pokes people at the bar who annoy her and throws books off bookshelves. Likewise John Fothergill, landlord of The Three Swans Hotel in Market Harborough, reputedly haunts his portrait on the premises, causing disturbances if it is removed.

The Anne of Cleves in Melton Mowbray dates back to 1384. This ancient building on the Burton Road was once a monk's chantry house. Its present-day patrons number the dead as well as the living, including a White Lady in the garden and a gentleman sitting on a bench near the back door. Ghost hunters have identified one of the several spirits as Alfred Syetys, a local axe murderer.

The Union Inn in Hinckley is reputedly haunted by a 'regular' who sits at his favourite table reading, as well as a mischievous child and several soldiers. Its cellar is haunted by a gentleman highwayman, who may well have met his end in the town square and was one of the bodies stored in the cellar.

The White Hart in Ashby de la Zouch was once used to detain prisoners due to be executed at the nearby castle. The White Hart was investigated by Spirit Team UK who detected phantom children and an elderly lady. Mysterious mist also manifests around the beer barrels and a spirit of indeterminate sex is often glimpsed. Its head hangs to one side, suggesting that it was hanged.

Plough Inn, Birstall. In the 1970s, it was reported that the pub cellar was haunted by a phantom barrel mover.

Renovations to the White Horse in Broughton Astley in 2011 set off a series of unearthly events. Soon after the old cellar floor was dug up, radios began to turn themselves on (even if they were unplugged), objects moved of their own accord or were thrown by unseen hands, and the attic doors opened. Black shadows were spotted in mirrors and the figure of a woman was seen about the otherwise empty pub.

The Woodman's Stroke, Rothley. Not all ghosts are sinister. The Woodman's resident spirit is called Gregory and those who spot him are said to be guaranteed good luck.

The Belper Arms, Newton Burgoland. This pub's male ghostly presence is notorious for slapping or stroking female waitresses – and trying to smother male waiters! The apparition only manifests at set times of the day – either 3.55 a.m. or 15.55 p.m. – earning him the nickname 'Five to four Fred'.

HAUNTED HOLY PLACES

Grace Dieu Priory

In the thirteenth century, Roesia de Verdun, an independent, wealthy landowner, built Grace Dieu Priory for the Augustan order of nuns so she could avoid remarriage by becoming its first prioress. The priory became the site of a hospital for local poor people until the Dissolution of the Monasteries.

Today, the priory lies in ruins, as does the Tudor house that was built after the dissolution. But it is not deserted. Various grey and white misty shapes have been sighted on and around the ruins, including a White Lady, who has been seen walking from the priory to the nearby bus stop. Several local bus drivers have been unnerved when they have stopped to take on a woman in white only to have her disappear as soon as the bus doors open to admit her!

Other encounters have been more sinister, with a council workman on the site refusing to work there again when he was pushed over by an invisible force.

Theories abound about the identity of the ghosts. Some state one is Agnes Litherland, a sixteenth-century abbess walled up in the priory after she gave birth to a child. But it could equally by a restless Roesia de Verdun, who is said to roam the grounds as a result of her grave being disturbed in the nineteenth century.

Switherland Rectory

Demolished after the First World War, Switherland Rectory was haunted by the daughter of its nineteenth-century rector. On returning home to prepare the house for the family, she was murdered by their drunken butler who then slit his own throat in remorse once he had sobered up.

Awful screams were said to be heard coming from the rectory at night, as well as alleged sightings of the ghostly butler, hacking at his throat.

After the demolition of the house, local legend tells that the figure of a lady in a grey dress, carrying a slab of stone from the rectory, was seen heading towards the church. The Grey Lady is now seen infrequently haunting the churchyard, mainly appearing around weddings, christenings and funerals.

Other Haunted Holy Places

St Margaret's Church, Leicester. A bell-ringing poltergeist and an old lady relocated to the church after their original haunt in the vicarage was demolished in the 1960s.

Church of St Edward King and Martyr, Castle Donington. In 1950, a brother and sister were visiting St Edward's when they got into a conversation with a vicar they did not know. The man explained his name was Father Dougal and that he had been based at the church in 1906. It was only later that the couple discovered that Father Dougal had indeed been vicar of the church – until his death in 1906.

Mount St Bernard's Abbey, Coalville. While exploring the abbey grounds in the 1990s, a woman visitor suddenly noticed a man behind her. He was quite unremarkable, with ginger hair and wearing a tan leather jacket. However, as he passed the lady he melted away into the shrubbery ahead.

PUBLIC BUILDINGS

The Guildhall, Leicester

Leicester's Guildhall has had a varied life. Since its construction in the fourteenth century, it has been the meeting house for the town guilds, the council house, police headquarters and prison. Now it is a museum. So it's no wonder it's credited with its fair share of ghosts – both human and animal. Locked doors in the mayor's parlour have been known to spring open of their own accord. A phantom cat and dog haunt the courtyard and great hall respectively and a tormented cavalier and the spirit of a policeman also roam the grounds.

A White Lady with a fondness for Deuteronomy 18.10 reputedly haunts the library. Curators regularly find the pages of the displayed bible turned to this passage, which relates to witchcraft and divination.

The Harborough Theatre, Market Harborough
Once the site of the Green Dragon Inn, this theatre has the reputation of being haunted by the spirit of an elderly sea captain who retired to the inn in his old age. Quite what an old sea dog was doing inland is unknown but his spirit is attached to his former residence and manifests as cold spots, disembodied voices and footsteps.

But the ghost could also be a former maid of the coaching inn called Hannah. This notorious flirt was supposedly murdered by her lover in a fit of rage. After a violent argument, the couple disappeared. Her lover was never seen again but Hannah's body was later discovered in the River Welland, 10 miles from the town.

Old Loughborough Magistrates' Court
Loughborough's old court also has its ghosts. Built in 1860 as a police station, it has sat empty since 2008. Footsteps and whispers have been heard about its abandoned rooms and corridors.

But the ghosts were active long before the building's abandonment. In the 1960s, a man spending the night in the cells struck up a conversation with the prisoner next door. When he was released the next day, he asked to say goodbye to his neighbour – only to be told the cell had been empty all night.

CASUALTIES OF WAR

Leicestershire has seen its fair share of battles and bloodshed throughout time. So it's no surprise that it also has its fair share of military ghostly goings-on.

Ghostly Invaders

Wigston Harcourt housing estate is partly built on a field called Heards Close. In the 1980s before the houses were built, a woman and her son spent an uncomfortable couple of nights camped on the site. On the first night, cries and moans were heard, as well as the clash of swords. The following evening, the woman was woken by what she initially thought was her son telling her to 'get up'. But on waking, she was greeted not by her own child but another, pale as a corpse and dressed in white.

Once the houses were built, residents saw a number of hazy figures marching in armour, before fading away at a nearby graveyard. In the 1880s, gravediggers had found fragments of broken shields, armour and swords, which were attributed to Danish invaders who pillaged Wigston in AD 876. Could it be that the site is haunted by this ghostly battle?

Bosworth Field, Sutton Cheney

Bosworth Field is arguably the county's most famous battlefield. The site of the Battle of Bosworth in 1485, it has a reputation for being haunted. Andrew James Wright in his book *Ghosts and Hauntings In and Around Leicestershire* cites a story from the 1980s when a group of visitors attended a steam rally on the site. One lady visitor began to feel most unusual. Despite the bright sunshine, she felt the day was cold and grey and began to talk to her companions about 'the hill'. Becoming very distressed, the lady asked for a horse. She could hear shouting and screaming and the sounds of battle. The hill she identified was Ambion Hill where the battle reputedly took place. Even more eerily, her experience occurred on 22 August – the anniversary of the battle.

Eerie Airmen

The British Shoe Corporation Warehouse at Scudmore Road, Braunston Firth, boasts the ghost of a Second World War RAF airman, seen fleeing in panic. The smell of burning often accompanies the spirit, mysteriously dissipating when he disappears. The apparition is supposedly the shade of the pilot of a plane that crashed at the site in 1942, when it was a wartime training facility.

Bottesford also boasts a similar haunting at its old RAF base, which closed at the end of the Second World War. Weird lights and the drone of plane engines have been heard and a solitary figure in a sheepskin flying jacket and flying helmet sighted near the control tower.

GHOSTS OF ROAD AND RAIL

School Lane

The residents of a terraced housing association property on School Lane in Loughborough never felt comfortable in their home. Soon after moving in, lights and the microwave began to inexplicably switch themselves on and off, and posters rearranged themselves on the walls.

The tenant contacted a medium who told her a ghost called Nigel, a man in his thirties with a low mental age, who was hidden away by his parents, haunted the property. But when ghostbuster Don Philips offered to investigate, he identified a further forty-nine spirits. Amongst these were a 6-year-old boy killed in a fire and a man who hanged himself in the cellar. Don managed to help most of the ghosts to find rest; but some remained.

Ley Lines

Frog Island in Leicester was once part of the town's abbey meadows before it became an island in the late eighteenth century,

after being annexed by the completion of the
Soar Canal.

The island quickly became a prime
location for textile mills in the nineteenth
century. But it was not until the 1970s that
the Britella Hosiery factory on New Pingle
Street manifested its ghost, a disruptive spirit
that caused much industrial unrest. An evil
presence was felt in the factory, with several people
being prodded by unseen fingers and a black mist
manifesting on the premises. The workers threatened
to strike because of the paranormal troublemaker so a
mild exorcism was carried out and the activity calmed down.

There is no clue as to the identity of the spirit, but the location
of the factory suggests a possible cause. 'Pingle' refers to an old
track. This could refer to the ley line that reputedly runs through
the street – with the Britella factory at its furthest end. Could it
be that the Britella ghost was no ghost at all but rather the power
of the Pingle Street ley line?

A Topsy-Turvy Ghost

In the mid-1990s, a motorist driving along Gibbet Lane in
Bilstone hit a large grey-haired man in a trench coat. The driver
stopped the car and checked for the injured man but he was
nowhere to be seen. The shocked driver called the police and a
search ensued, but the mystery man was not to be found.

Others have seen a similar ghost. Is he John Massey, known as
Topsy-Turvy, whose body was displayed in the lane's eponymous
gibbet? Massey was a violent drunk who drowned his wife and
nearly killed her young daughter in the early nineteenth century.
He was hung at Red Hill in Birstall but his body was returned to
the parish the murder was committed in and displayed in a gibbet.

But if Massey does not haunt the area, it is possible his victims
do. In 1979, a motorist saw two figures staring at the gibbet post
– the dripping wet figures of a woman and young girl.

Ghostly Train Spotting

The old line at Thorpe Sackville was where a dog walker spotted the ghostly remnants of an early railway outing. The woman briefly glimpsed the vision of a train with a tall smokestack and three carriages, surrounded by men in top hats and ladies in crinolines, chatting happily, before they faded away.

Mary Quinn

Harry Gamble was a bus conductor on the number 616 that ran from St Margaret's bus station in Leister to Uppingham, a small town in Rutland. Harry noticed that a pretty young lady who got off at the village of Tugby was becoming a regular passenger. She told Harry her name was Mary Quinn and that she lived with her parents in a cottage with a blue, leaded window door surrounded by roses.

One day, it rained hard. Mary was only wearing a light summer dress, so Harry lent her his raincoat so she could return home unscathed. He never saw her again..

Disturbed by her sudden disappearance, Harry went to Tugby on his day off to see if he could find her. He located her house by its description. But when he mentioned Mary's name to the lady who opened the door, she slammed it in his face, much distressed.

A puzzled Harry called out to a neighbour to find out what he had done wrong. The man led him to the local graveyard, where he was shown a gravestone dedicated to Mary Quinn. The date of death was two years earlier. What was more, draped over the back of the stone was Harry's coat.

Other Ghosts of Road and Rail

Rothley Station is reputedly haunted by its former stationmaster and a ghostly dog and its owner – both killed on the line just before the start of the Second World War. A phantom woman in blue also haunts the station waiting room.

In 1967 and 1994, witnesses at Belvoir Castle Rally Track, Denton, saw a mounted figure on horseback, dressed in a long grey coat and believed to be a highwayman.

In 2009, a startled driver on the M1 at Castle Donington spotted a man dressed in a green jacket, dark trousers and with something on his head standing in the middle lane of the M1 motorway, just past junction 21. When she glanced back in her rearview mirror, to check if the man was OK, she found he had completely disappeared.

Platform One of Loughborough Central Station is said to be haunted by a transparent railway worker, dressed in an old-fashioned uniform, holding an oil lamp.

ALLOTMENTS AND GARDENS

The former site of the Baggy Marsh Allotments on Newton Lane, Wigston, used to be haunted by an old gardener. Neglectful allotmenteers would often feel his wrath. One was badly stung by wasps that appeared in a nest in his shed. Another's water butt reputedly dried up overnight, while a further unfortunate stuck a fork in his foot – all apparently at the behest of the otherwise benign ghost who manifested as a pipe-smoking old man, dressed in baggy trousers, tied at the knee with string, a baggy coat and cloth cap.

Famous Ghosts
The ruins of Lady Jane Grey's former home on Bradgate Park are reputedly visited by the doomed queen's spirit every Christmas when she makes the journey from the old church to the ruins of the house in a carriage.

John of Gaunt is said to haunt Leicester Castle, reputedly the favourite of his many residences.

Even before his grave was discovered on the site of the Greyfriar's friary in Leicester, the ghost of Richard III was said to roam the streets in the neighbourhood. But the dead king's spirit may also have turned up elsewhere in Leicestershire: at Donington le Heath manor house where he spent the night before the fateful Battle of Bosworth.

Amateur paranormal researchers apparently recorded the king's voice in 2013. A spirit was contacted in the room and when asked, 'What's your name?' it replied 'Richard'.

GHOSTLY MISCELLANEA

The Bleeding Gravestone
The spirit of Richard Smith, a young saddler killed by a recruiting sergeant in 1727, was said to haunt a tree in Hinckley.

Smith was watching the sergeant on Duck Puddle Lane as he attempted to lure new recruits for the army. He kept calling out and correcting the sergeant (for instance, pointing out that the local pub was not named 'The George' after the king but instead the saint). As the saddler showed up more of the sergeant's ignorance, the crowd began to jeer and the solider lost his temper. He turned upon the young saddler and ran him through with his halberd, pinning him to a nearby oak tree.

Every April, the saddler's friends visited his grave – and reputedly blood-red moisture would ooze from the headstone.

The Lost Wife of Blaby
One April night in 1995, at around 8.30 p.m., two people driving to a party stopped for a smoke in their car. While taking their break, they saw the outline of a woman in a long coat walking near a steep bank.

Turning on the car's headlights to check the woman was all right, they found the figure was nowhere to be seen. Thinking no more of it, they finished their cigarettes and carried on to the party.

Towards the end of the evening, people began to tell ghost stories. One of them included the tale of a phantom woman who was said to be searching for the ghost of her husband who drowned in 1923. The spot was the very place the partygoers had stopped.

Abbey Pumping Station Museum

The former pumping station near to the National Space Centre is reputedly haunted by the ghost of a worker who fell to his death in the beam engine house. The ethereal engineer makes his presence felt by playing with the lights and making noises in the basement.

The Miller of Kibworth

Once, a local miller of Kibworth entered into a drinking contest at a local pub. Fearful that the miller would win, his companions laced his drinks with gin – rendering the miller deeply unconscious. The miller could not be roused and gave no signs of life, and so he was duly declared dead and buried. But soon afterwards, noises were heard from his grave that suggested the unfortunate miller had in fact been merely sleeping off his very heavy session – only to awake in the most horrible and lethal of circumstances. His spirit has often been seen wandering about the graveyard.

FOOD AND DRINK

FRUIT AND VEG

'Bean Belly Leicestershire'

'Shake a Leicestershire man by the collar and you may hear the beans rattle in his belly' (Magna Britannia, *1820*)

Leicestershire was once known for its prolific cultivation of beans – particularly the broad bean, which was the staple of many a country diet. So prolific was the bean in the Leicestershire diet that the county was known as 'Bean Belly Leicestershire'.

The popularity of beans as a staple crop and favourite food led to some of the major places of cultivation being named after them – such as the village of Barton in the Beans, near Hinckley and Bosworth.

Fruits: Old and New

The rich clay soils of Leicestershire make them the perfect place to grow apples and there are plenty of local varieties. Baback orange and croft sharp, Belvoir seedling and Packington Apple are favourite local varieties, as is the Annie Elizabeth Cooking Apple.

This sweet apple has a sad story behind its name. Samuel Greatorex, a magistrate's clerk of Leicester, developed it in 1857. But the apple had to wait for its name until 1866 – when Greatorex used it to immortalise the name of his deceased illegitimate baby daughter.

The 'Syston White Plum' is a well-known county variety, grown since the late 1800s. Oval, with a thin yellow skin, it is harvested in September and famed as a dessert plum and the symbol of Syston.

Oadby and Wigston have hosted an Apple Day for about six years, promoting Leicestershire's apple varieties. Held at Brocks Hill Park, the event celebrates all things apple: from juice to honey, cider and the Leicestershire Heritage Apple Project.

Naturally tomatoes are not native to Leicestershire but the county has its own heritage tomato. The George Nursery at Blaby grew the Blaby Special from 1912. It was much favoured by local people for its bright red colour and juicy flesh. During the Second World War it was especially popular and locals would queue for up to half a mile for their chance to acquire the tomato treat. But the farm went out of business after the war and the Blaby Special was lost. That is, until the seeds were rediscovered in a seed bank in the Netherlands.

In 2006, the people of Blaby were reunited with their tomato and they have been growing it on their allotments ever since. To celebrate the return of their favourite fruit, since August 2010 Blaby has held its own annual tomato festival.

FAMOUS FOODS AND LOCAL RECIPES

Cheese

Stilton is probably the most famous cheese of the county, known as 'The King of English Cheeses' because of its full-bodied fragrance and delicate veins of blue mould.

There are various origin stories for Stilton. One attributes its creation to a Mrs Pawlet, a Wymondham cheesemaker who in 1730 made a cream cheese, which she sent to a relative, Cooper Thornhill, the landlord of The Bell Inn in Stilton, Huntingdon.

The cheese became popular with the inn's customers and was soon known as Stilton Cheese after the village it was sold in. The Bell Inn was situated along the main London to Edinburgh Road – ensuring that Stilton's reputation soon spread the length of the country.

Another story credits Quenby Hall as the birthplace of Stilton, where it was reputedly known as Lady Beaumont's cheese. Yet another claims the cheese was the original creation of a Mrs Orton of Little Dalby.

In fact, historical research confirms some elements of the legends – but also proves that Stilton evolved over time, rather than being the product of any one individual. Stilton was indeed named after the place it was originally distributed from, however, it was being produced in Leicestershire long before 1730. It may even date back to the fourteenth century.

Richard Bradley published a recipe for a hard cream cheese, pressed and boiled in its whey like Stilton, in a newsletter in 1723. Daniel Defoe in his *Tours Through the villages of England and Wales* also knew of it, referring to it in 1724 as 'The English Parmesan'.

It seems that Thornhill actually commissioned Mrs Pawlet to make the cheese for him in 1743 – when a trade for it had already been established. Mrs Pawlet subsequently recruited other cheesemakers to work with her, using her recipe for a blue-veined cheese – the same recipe we know today.

Until the nineteenth century, all Stilton was produced within 20 miles of Melton Mowbray. Today, true Stilton is only produced in six dairies, one being Webster's Dairy in Saxelbye. In 1969, it was one of the few cheeses granted a Protected Designation of Origin by the European Commission.

Red Leicester is a millstone-shaped farmhouse cheese originally known as the Leicestershire cheese until the 'red' – caused by the addition of extract of carrots to distinguish it from other local cheeses – was added to the name in the seventeenth century.

Red Leicester reached London via Leicester's famous May and October cheese fairs. Like Stilton, it quickly became popular in the capital and by the mid eighteenth century was a firm favourite.

These days, food dye rather than carrots creates the cheese's distinct orange colour but the cheese still maintains its mellow flavour. Only two dairies in Leicestershire produce the traditional variety of Red Leicester, one being Sparkenhoe Farm at Upton near Market Bosworth.

Pies and Snacks

The Melton Mowbray Pork Pie was actually a by-product of Leicestershire's cheese industry. Whey left over from cheese making was a perfect pig food. This encouraged the people of Melton Mowbray, in particular, to keep them as livestock.

The abundance of pork made it a staple food for labourers. It was made into the perfect portable packed lunch by baking the meat in a disposable pastry pot.

By the late eighteenth century, foxhunting was an integral part of Melton country life and the local landed gentry became curious about the pies consumed by their grooms and servants.

And so the pork pie went mainstream. The local huntsmen began to buy them from shops in Melton town. In 1831, enterprising Melton baker, Edward Adcock, having noted that the local gentry were lapping the pies up, decided to market them in London.

Soon, demand was such that other businesses were following suit. The hot water pastry, which was originally little more than a disposable wrapping, became an integral part of the dish. It was shaped around a bottle or wooden dolly, before the filling of uncured pork and bone stock jelly was packed in.

Today the pie continues to be made around Melton: hand formed and from uncured pork. Ye Olde Pork Pie Shoppe in Melton Mowbray was established in 1851. Now owned by Dickenson and Morris, it is the last firm in Melton to bake authentic pork pies on the premises. Like Stilton, the Melton Mowbray Pork Pie has been granted Protected Geographical Status by the EU.

But while its adoption by the landed gentry ensured its national fame, the pork pie is still a Leicestershire favourite – quite often for breakfast.

Pies in general seem to be a Leicestershire favourite. In 1963, Trevor Storey began selling pies made to his wife's own recipes to chip shops and football stadiums.

Trevor's pies became a firm and lucrative favourite, leading to him setting up a factory for mass production and renaming his company Pukka Pies Ltd. Some 60 million pies are made daily at the company's Leicester factory, employing 300 local people.

The pork pie is not the only Leicestershire favourite to evolve through necessity. Walkers Crisps were produced by local butchers, the Walker family, whose business had been established in Leicester from the 1880s. Meat rationing in the Second World War saw trade drop, so Walkers looked for alternative ways to make money by tapping into the rising popularity of potato crisps as a popular snack. Some 47 per cent of all British crisps are now produced under the Walkers brand at their factory in Leicester.

Cakes and Sweets

Whetstone Cakes are a Leicestershire specialty made with caraway seeds and rosewater. The recipe was first recorded in 1741.

But older still is the Bosworth Jumble, reputedly baked for Richard III to take to the Battle of Bosworth. The dough was made from butter, sugar, eggs and flour and flavoured with either caraway seeds, aniseed or almond before being shaped into a knot and boiled before baking.

Richard lost the battle and the cakes – which were reputedly liberated and eaten by his rival Henry Tudor. From then onwards, the jumbles were baked in an 'S' shape in honour of the victor – using the recipe found in the dead hand of Richard's own cook.

'Jumble' comes from the Latin for twin, *gemmel*, which explains the cake's symmetrical shape rather better than the defeat of one king by another.

Leicestershire also has its own form of cheesecakes although they are not recognised as such by the rest of the country.

Leicestershire cheesecakes are small pastry tarts filled with sweetened curd cheese and dried fruit. The tarts could well have been made as early as the Middle Ages, as the accounts of Eleanor, Countess of Leicester and wife of Simon de Montfort mentions 'cheese in tarts'. Nowadays, the cakes have to be marketed as curd cakes to avoid confusion with the more traditional cheesecake with the biscuit base. But Leicestershire locals stubbornly refuse to refer to them as such. To them, the little tarts are the definitive cheesecakes.

Sand cakes are another traditional Leicestershire cake. Loaf shaped, they are made from a mix of wheat flour and corn flour or potato flour that gives them the sandy texture that also earns them their name. Sometimes served topped with a lemon icing, the sand cake used to be a favourite for dessert, especially when served with fruit and cream.

Foxes Glacier Mints were developed by a local Leicester grocer in the late nineteenth century. Walter Fox originally established the company in a Leicester warehouse in 1880. In 1918, the famous mints were first developed: clear, minty ice cube shapes that remain popular today.

The trademark of the mints was Peppy the polar bear. Local artist and illustrator of the Thomas the Tank engine books, Reginald Dalby, designed the famous polar bear motif.

THE ORIGINS OF AFTERNOON TEA

Whilst visiting Belvoir Castle in the 1840s, Anna Russell, seventh Duchess of Bedford, found that the space between luncheon at midday and dinner at 8 p.m. left her feeling extremely peckish in the afternoon.

So, in order not to offend her hosts, the duchess had servants sneak her up some tea with bread and butter at mid-afternoon to sustain her between meals. She continued this secret ritual throughout her stay – and also began to invite other, select lady guests to join her. This 'small and select' group of afternoon diners gathered in her rooms, tempted by the tea, which had developed to include small sandwiches and cakes.

The ladies and the duchess herself took their new, illicit habit back to London with them where it was served out in the open. And so afternoon tea quickly became an established practice – in middle- and upper-class houses at least.

CAPTAIN SCOTT'S EXPEDITION

In 1901, Market Harborough company W. Symington supplied Captain Scott's ill-fated Antarctic expedition with its dried goods of pea flour and pea soup. Fifty years later, one of the expedition's food stores was rediscovered – and Symington's pea flour was still in perfect condition.

MILLS

Claybrooke Mill in Claybrooke Magna is one of the only commercial watermills in Leicestershire still producing flour. The current mill dates to 1763, but milling has taken place on the site for the last 1,000 years. Today, Claybourne produces a range of forty traditional and modern flours such as chilli flour mix and spicy tomato flour mix.

TERMS FOR FOOD

Leicestershire folk have their own particular names for many everyday types of food and drink. Here are just a few examples:

Bungole – cheese
Cob – roll or bap
Rocks – sweets
Guzgogs – gooseberries
Oakey – ice cream
Snaps – lunch
Council pop – tap water
Toggly – buttered toast

CURRY

The first curry restaurant in Leicestershire, The Taj Mahal, was founded on Highfields Street, Leicester, in 1960.

Its owner, Nor Ahmed, had moved to the city just after the Second World War. He found himself one of only twenty other Asians in the whole city. So from the start, his restaurant depended on enticing English diners, as well as giving his expatriate friends a taste of home.

The last owner of the restaurant, Ali Asraf, remembers the initial English reaction to this new, exotic food. 'People were very scared it would be very hot,' he said.

But clearly they liked it, for curry took off in a big way across the whole county. In 2007, Leicester was declared curry capital of Britain with Belgrave Road the place for a real Leicester curry. The Taj Mahal itself remained open for fifty-five years before its sad closure in 2015.

Curry has also married itself with more traditional Leicester food. McIndians, established in 1989, with its cheeky by-line 'You've tried the cowboys, now try the Indians', have spiced up traditional takeaway favourites such as burgers and fish and chips.

Asian food in Leicestershire is big business in more than just restaurants. Fifteen major Indian food manufacturers are located in the county. The Leicester Bakery Ltd is one of the largest specialist bread producers in the UK – commercially producing naan and pitta breads. Founded in 1977 by Mohamed Sabat to sell pitta bread across the Midlands, in 1984 it expanded its operations to launch handmade naans and chapattis. Mayur Foods, another Asian-run Leicestershire company, crafts naans, chapattis and pittas the traditional way in tandoori ovens for distribution across the whole country.

Belgrave's Golden Mile

For a truly unique experience of Asia within Leicestershire, a visit to Leicester's Golden Mile along Belgrave Road is a must. Vibrant and full of the sounds and smells of another continent, the first Asian shops began to open along it in the early 1970s. One of the first was an Asian supermarket called Uppkar, which specialised in selling Asian fruits and vegetables.

But there is much more to Leicestershire's world food than just curry. Tapas, Italian, Chinese, Greek, Arabic French and Afro-Caribbean cuisine are all represented – especially in the city of Leicester where its world-famous market sells all the ingredients to prepare your own.

BILTONG AND BANGERS

W. Archer & Sons, butchers on Queen's Road, have developed a new Leicestershire favourite: South African biltong.

Biltong is high in protein and low in carbs – which explains why the Archers version is so popular with local sportsmen as well as the local South African ex-pats – one of whom was the inspiration for the butcher's venture: 'An Afrikaans student came in one day, about four years ago, and said he wanted some beef to make his own biltong at home,' explained owner Shaun in an interview with the *Leicester Mercury*. 'He made me some and I thought it would be great to start making my own and selling it in the shop.'

In fact, so good are the butcher's South African goodies that ex-Leicester Tigers player Dan Hipkiss still weekly receives 2kg dehydrated deliveries of his favourite biltong now that he has moved 120 miles away to play for Bath – which he shares with his South African team mates.

MARKETS AND FOOD FESTIVALS

Melton Mowbray has been a market town for over 1,000 years. Recorded as Leicestershire's only market in the 1086 Domesday survey, it is the third oldest market in England. Tuesday has been market day ever since royal approval was given in 1324.

The town itself is known as 'The Rural Capital of Food' and since 2009 has been the host of The British Pie awards that celebrates all varieties of British pies – not just the pork pie!

The annual East Midlands Food & Drink Festival held in Melton Mowbray had over 200 exhibitors and 20,000 visitors attend in 2007, making it the largest British regional food festival.

Loughborough, Market Harborough and Hinckley also have long-established markets. Market Harborough's has been in service since 1219, Loughborough's since 1221 and Hinckley market is 700 years old and was voted best outdoor market in 2010.

Leicester market is also 700 years old. It is the largest covered marketplace in Europe, selling a wide variety of fruit and vegetables from across the world, as well as meat and fish, fresh spices and general haberdashery. It was voted Britain's favourite market in 2011 and is home to some 300 businesses.

LIQUID REFRESHMENT

Beer

Everards Brewery is the county's largest brewer, producing beers such as the famous Tiger, Old Original and Everards Bitter.

'No effort shall be found wanting in the production and supply of genuine ale of a first rate quality,' said its founder William Everard in 1849, when he set up the first brewery with his brother Thomas.

By 1896, the company had expanded to Burton on Trent. Tigers Brewery was founded in 1901 and is still based in Leicester today. The brewery remains in the Everard family and has 175 pubs about the county.

Other local breweries include:

The Belvoir Brewery, Old Dalby
The Parish Brewery, Burrough on the Hill
The Gas Dog Brewery, Somerby
The Pig Pub Brewery, Claybourne Magna

Notable Pubs and Hostelries

The Belper Arms in Newton Burgoland dates back to 1290 when it was known as The Shepherd and Shepherdess Inn. It is the oldest pub in Leicestershire.

The oldest pub in Leicester is The Bowling Green on Oxford Street that dates to the 1700s. In the 1990s its name was changed to The Polar Bear to commemorate the motif of Fox's glacier mints, but recently it has reverted to its original name.

When Henry VIII parted from his fourth wife, one of his many gifts was a pretty house in Melton Mowbray. Today it is a pub, The Anne of Cleves, named in honour of its former owner.

The former home of the Everard family became a pub – The Stamford Arms – in 1921. But according to Groby Heritage Group, the tall chimney of the pub used to belong to a quarry.

The Man Within Compass in Whitwick is unique for its name, which is of uncertain origin and not found anywhere else in England. But it is known to the locals as The Rag and Mop –for equally obscure reasons.

The Bull Inn, Donnington, once played host to Laurel and Hardy. Stan Laurel's sister was the landlady and the comedy duo stayed there for Christmas 1952 while they were appearing at the Empire Theatre in Nottingham.

Mineral Water

Mineral water is not just a modern phenomenon. In the nineteenth century, Leicestershire was well known for its mineral waters – and still produces it to this day.

The Charnwood Hills are a source of exceptionally pure water, which explains why the Switherland Water Company grew up in the area and still flourishes.

But it was not the area's only producer of mineral water. Whitwick was once home to three mineral water factories, the largest of which, Bernard Beckworth on Cademan Street, ran from 1875 to the 1970s. Horace Stinsons was more short-lived, running only from 1912–28, while Massey's of Castle Street only lasted from 1916–41.

SPORT AND LEISURE

SPORT ...

Cock Fighting

In 1849, cockfighting was declared illegal. Up until that point, it was a favourite sport in Leicestershire.

Initially, it was the preserve of the well-to-do. In 1595, Elizabethan spectators in Leicester laid out 21 shillings and 4 pence for sweet wine, cherries, cake and bread for the 'gentlemen' spectators. The match in question took place in a purpose-built roofed pit, somewhere between Halford and Granby Street.

Melton Mowbray also had its own purpose-built pit, just behind the Anne of Cleves public house. So many people would attend during the Croxton Park race week that a new pit was built in 1825 to accommodate 500 spectators.

Another reason that matches were the preserve of the gentry were the huge sums bet at them – sometimes between 50 to 500 guineas. Inter-county matches even occurred. The *Leicester and Nottingham Journal* of 1768 advertised a fight between 'the gentlemen of Leicestershire and the gentlemen of Nottinghamshire, to shew and weigh 21 cocks for the main sand to fight for two guineas a battle.'

'The Best Hunting Ground in England'

Leicestershire is considered to be the birthplace of foxhunting – so much so that the fox is the county symbol, adorning not only the county coat of arms but the emblems of its county cricket club and Leicester City Football Club.

It wasn't until the eighteenth century that foxhunting developed as a sport, rather than a way of culling 'vermin'. Key to its rise was the enclosure of land. Open land was being portioned off into smaller, separate fields that were easier to farm. This reduced the open ground available to the deer population, leading to its decline.

Less deer meant less deerstalking. So the landed gentry needed to find another way to amuse themselves. The first man believed to own a pack of foxhounds in England was Thomas Boothby of Tolley Park near Desford, who established his pack in 1696. But the 'father of foxhunting' was Hugh Meynell, who took over from Boothby as master of the Quorn hunt in 1753 and remained in post until 1800.

In 1753, when he was 18, Meynell began to experiment with a new breed of hound at his estate of Quorndon Hall. His hounds were faster and had more stamina. So, in order to use them to their full potential, they needed a faster kind of hunt.

Since the Middle Ages, it had been traditional for hunting to occur in the morning, when foxes and other wild creatures were slowed down by their nightly feed. But Meynell wanted more of a challenge for his new breed of dogs, a challenge that would make hunting more exciting (for the hunters at least!). So he introduced the mid-morning meet. By this time, the fox would have digested its nightly meal, making it lighter on its feet and more of a challenge to catch. Fences between the sections of enclosed land added an extra dimension and so the modern hunt was born.

Strange Sports Past and Present

The Whipping Toms

The custom of the Whipping Toms at Leicester's Shrove Tuesday Fair began as a primitive game of hockey, with two teams of men and boys playing to score in goals at either end of The Newarke. At 1 p.m., the match would end and three men in blue smocks carrying wagon whips and bells would clear the players away.

By the early nineteenth century, the custom had 'evolved'. Instead, at 1 p.m. a bell rang to clear away the patrons of the Shrove Tuesday Fair. Anyone in the know would quit the area very quickly, for if they did not, or they were not prepared to pay a fine of *2d* (or pad their legs), they would be victims of the Whipping Toms. For now, instead of hitting a ball, the Toms struck any unlucky trespasser to their area about the legs. The violence and disorder of the 'game' was such that in 1846 Leicester's corporation obtained an Act of Parliament to bring the 'sport' to an end.

Extreme Ironing

Leicester is the birthplace of a little-known sporting phenomenon: Extreme Ironing, 'the latest danger sport that combines the thrills of an extreme outdoor activity with the satisfaction of a well-pressed shirt' according to the Extreme Ironing Bureau.

In 1997, Leicester resident Phil Shaw was contemplating the drudgery of the mundane chore after a hard day at work and decided to make it more fun by combining it with his passion for rock climbing.

It worked for Phil. Calling himself 'Steam', he began touring in 1999 to promote his new sport. Extreme Ironing is now especially popular in Germany, the USA, New Zealand, Australia, South Africa and Fiji. Participants don't limit themselves to rocks: activities such as skiing, canoeing, marathon running, sky and scuba diving have been conjoined with the iron and the ironing board.

In 2002, the British team won gold and bronze at the first World Extreme Ironing Championships.

Football
In the Middle Ages, football was considered a nuisance game, played in the streets to the inconvenience of all but the players. In 1467 and 1488, it was even outlawed in Leicester by order of its Corporation. The sport's reputation did not improve. In 1592, its players in Oadby were referred to as 'abandoned persons'.

The custom of bottle kicking every Easter Monday at Hallerton may be a survival of an early form of football. Every year, teams from Hallerton and the neighbouring village of Medbourne gather at Hallerton's 'hare pie bank' – a piece of land bequeathed to the Church for so long as the bottle kicking occurred – for something that is a cross between an impromptu rugby/football match.

Originally, two hare pies are cut into pieces and distributed amongst the crowd. Teams then kick two large 5kg wooden bottles hooped with iron, and containing ale, between the village boundaries. Goals are a mile apart, meaning the resulting scramble occurrs over fences, fields and streams. The winner is decided by the best of three bottles, meaning the 'match' could go on all day!

Leicester Fosse Football Club was formed in 1884 by former pupils of Wyggeston's School in a garden shed on Fosse Road. Their first game occurred that same year, with a team from Syston. The Fosse won 5-0.

The following year, the burgeoning team established its headquarters on Victoria Park. During this period, the team colours were brown and blue, rather than the white and blue of today.

But as with other Leicester sports, Victoria Park was just a stopping point for the Fosse. In 1887 the club moved to the cycle and cricket ground on Belgrave Road. There they stayed, until Leicester Tigers outbid them for the ground. However, in 1891 they settled at a new, permanent home at Filbert Street.

In 1890, the Fosse entered the FA cup for the first time, losing 4-0 to Burton Wanderers. These early years were not successful ones and they finished bottom of the football league in 1903/04.

But better days were ahead. In 1913, the Fosse were 5,000-1 outsiders to win the FA Cup. They finished tied with Norwich

City, the finish of what captain Wes Morgan described as 'a real underdog story.'

In 1919, the team changed their name. Leicester had just regained its city status, so Leicester Fosse became Leicester City. The newly named team continued on the up. In 1949, they reached the FA Cup Final – but lost 3-1 to Wolves.

1969 was the penultimate time the team played in the final – until 2016 when the club won the premier league following Tottenham's 2-2 draw with Chelsea. A fitting ending to the 'real underdog story' to date.

Leicester City has been the starting point in the careers of a number of famous footballers, including England player and TV sports commentator Gary Linekar, who began playing for his home team in 1977, turning professional in 1978, and one of England's greatest goalkeepers, Peter Shilton, who was born in Leicester and also honed his skills at Leicester City.

But it's not just The Foxes who have scored big. In 1894, Loughborough Town Football Club beat Aston Villa 2-1. The man of the match was star player Albert Carnelly. Albert was famous for his flatcap, which he wore when playing. It was said if he took it off, a goal would be scored.

Rugby

Leicester Tigers are the most successful English Rugby club since the beginning of rugby league.

The club was founded in 1880 along Belgrave Road in Leicester. Their nickname was coined in 1885, from the team's original brown and yellow kit – and possibly the local regiment, who had served time in India and who and were also known as the Tigers.

The Tigers made various switches in the 1890s. Firstly, they changed home, establishing themselves in 1892 at the Welford Road site they still occupy today. The terms of renewal on their new lease at Belgrave Road was unacceptable, so they agreed terms with Leicester's Corporation and signed a ten-year lease on a parcel of land sandwiched between Welford and Aylestone Roads.

In fact, it was in a much better position for the club, being nearer the town centre. In all, it cost £1,100 to prepare and the new ground opened in grand style on 16 September 1892 when the Tigers played against the Leicestershire XV. They won 17-0.

In 1895, the club switched kit, opting for the current scarlet, green and white strip. But they still remained the Tigers.

Two years later, the team had their first major win – The Midlands County Cup, which they proceeded to win every year until 1905. The Tigers then dropped out to 'give other teams a chance'!

By the late twentieth century, the team was going from strength to strength. Supporter numbers were on the increase and coaches such as Chalkie White ensured that the wins were too. In 1997, six Leicester players were selected to play in the British Lion's tour of South Africa and between 1998 and 2002, the team won the premiership title four years in a row, as well as becoming the first team to win the European Cup successively.

The Tigers won the Heineken Cup in 2001, were European champions in 2002, English champions from 2000–02 and 2006–10 and top of the Rugby premiership in 2010.

Notable Leicestershire rugby players include:

Dorian West – Rugby footballer, Rugby World Cup winner.
Martin Johnson CBE – Former rugby union player and England international; played for Leicester Tigers from 1989–2006.
Martin Corry – Rugby union player with 279 appearances for Leicester Tigers and 64 for England.

Cricket
The first recorded cricket match in Leicestershire occurred in Barrow upon Soar in 1744. In the days before factories, the

sport was especially popular with framework knitters who had weekends free to practice the game.

Cricket quickly spread across the county, becoming an important village sport, popular at Hathern, Long Whatton, Shepshed, Loughborough, Hinckley, Lutterworth, Wigston and Fleckney. In Melton Mowbray the cricket season went on until October every year.

Players began to compete against other clubs: some local, such as Nottingham, with others as far afield as London. Loughborough hosted the first inter-county match against Nottingham, while in Barwall the annual match against Coventry and North Warwickshire has been ongoing since 1807.

In 1820, the Leicestershire and Rutland Cricket Club was formed. But the club lacked a home ground. Leicestershire initially used St Margaret's pasture for fixtures, followed in 1825 by the Wharf Street ground, which was considered the finest cricket pitch in England. Sadly, the land was sold for building in 1860.

By 1872, the club had relocated to Victoria Park. Many matches were played there but the cost of enclosing the cricketing area for games was expensive. A new, permanent home was required.

In 1877, for the sum of £40,000, 16 acres of land was purchased along Aylestone Road. A sports complex was constructed, with an athletics ground, hotel for visitors and a 12-acre cricket pitch, which took up the lion's share of the space.

The new ground was initially known as 'The Aylestone Ground' but it was renamed Grace Road shortly afterwards. Many believe this is after the famous cricketer W.G. Grace: in fact, it was after a local property owner.

The first match at the new pitch was held on 22 April 1878, between the Leicestershire XI and a visiting Australian team, the 22 Colts. Thirty thousand people – still a record number to this day – watched Leicestershire beat the Aussies.

Swimming

Jenny Fletcher of Belgrave was known as 'The world's first great woman swimmer'. She was an undefeated swimming champion between 1906 and 1909, setting eleven world records, earning six Champion of England medals and an Olympic gold.

Boxing

In the early nineteenth century, boxing was illegal and unregulated. But that did not prevent its popularity – especially amongst the upper classes. Even the king was a boxing fan!

The first ever prize bareknuckle boxing match was held at Wymondham in Leicestershire on 28 September 1811 between Tom 'The Moor' Molyneux, a freed slave from America, and Tom Crib of England.

The choice of venue was cunning, situated as it was on the boundary of Leicestershire, Rutland and Lincolnshire. The match was illegal so the 15–20,000 spectators could avoid arrest by the magistrates of one county by crossing over into one of the others – even though many of the spectators were local officials themselves!

The match lasted just twenty minutes, with Crib winning in the eleventh round by knocking Molyneux unconscious. The winner walked away with a prize of a cup, £2,600 – and a broken jaw.

Notable Leicestershire boxers include:

- Market Harborough's Jack Gardner, who represented Britain in the 1948 London Olympics before going on to become British, British Empire and European Heavy Weight Champion.
- Rendall Munroe. Leicester born and based, Munroe is the WBA International Super Bantamweight Champion and has also held commonwealth titles.
- Chris Pyatt. The former World Middleweight Champion boxer may be Islington born but he has made Leicester his home.

Horse Racing

The first horse race in Leicestershire was recorded at Leicester in 1603 on the Abbey Meadows – the town's first racecourse. The racing conditions were less than ideal. The land was liable to flooding by the nearby River Soar and races were something of a struggle for the horses that often had to wade knee deep to the finish line.

So in 1742, the course moved to St Mary's Field in Leicester's South Fields. However, this too was liable to flooding – with the added disadvantage of four turnpike roads to interrupt the races. Therefore, the races moved to what is now Victoria Park, which was at least dry and open. And there they stayed until 1883, when the sport moved to its current home in Oadby.

Famous Racehorses and Their Trainers

The 1914 Grand National winner Sunlock was trained in Loughborough. His owner was local man Thomas Tyler who trained the horse behind the Brush Works. Sunlock was a 100-1 outsider – until the locals began to back him, shattering the odds. His win meant the lucky punters of Loughborough raked in £10,000 between them.

The thoroughbred Burrough Hill Lad was named by owner Stan Riley after the Leicester hill and village of his birth. Trained by Jenny Pitman, he competed in a total of forty-two races, half of which he won, including victories in 1984 at the Cheltenham Gold Cup, Hennessy Gold Cup and King George VI.

Jenny Pitman herself was born and bred in Leicestershire and the first woman to train a Grand National winner, Corbiere, in 1983. Jenny came from a family of horse trainers, married jockey Richard Pitman and established her own point-to-point yard which became a first class institution, producing her first win in 1975.

Donington Park Racing Circuit
The first permanent racing park in England, Donington Park, was established after the First World War by Fred Craner, a motorcycle rider. Craner approached the owner of Donington Hall and persuaded him to allow him to use the roads on the Donington estate for racing.

The first race took place on Whit Monday 1931 on a track that was 2 miles and 327 yards or 3,518m in length. It was such a success that by 1933 Craner had permission to build a permanent trackway.

Once built, the racecourse was used for motor racing. The first was the Donington Park Trophy Race held on 7 October 1933. The first Donington Grand Prix was in 1935.

The racetrack fell into disuse after it was converted into a military vehicle depot during the Second World War. But in 1971, Tom Wheatcroft brought the land and revived the circuit and on 28 May 1977 Donington finally reopened.

Since then, the site has hosted both motor racing and speedway events including the British Touring Car Championship, British Superbike Championship, the 1993 European Grand Prix and the 2006 World Series. But loss of the rights to host the British Grand Prix and British Superbike Championships has once again led to the track's decline.

Notable Leicestershire racing drivers include speedway racer Fred Wilkinson, who raced for England vs. Australia, and ran Lansdowne Garage in Syston, and Formula One driver Roger Williamson. Born in Ashby de la Zouch, Williamson tragically died during the 1973 Dutch Grand Prix.

... AND LEISURE

Traditional Leicestershire Festivals

Yearly Fairs

In the days before cinemas and theatres, fairs provided seasonal bouts of entertainment in Leicestershire. Every town and village held at least one annually. At its peak, Leicester held six.

Fairs were places of food, drink, games and curiosities. Humberstone Gate Fair, held every May in Leicester, epitomizes their spirit. The *Leicester Journal* describes how the site was originally a piece of waste ground on the south side of Humberstone Gate. Entrance prices varied according to social standing: 1 shilling for ladies and gentlemen, sixpence for tradesmen and 3 pence for work people.

Animals such as zebras and the 'kangaroo rat from Botany Bay' were on show, along with sword swallowers, fire-eaters, Irish giants, dwarfs, armless ladies, wrestlers, tumblers and tricksters. The fair was opened by a proclamation at the High Cross followed by a procession led by the mayor.

When the last fair was held in 1904, the *Leicester Guardian* applauded the end of an 'annoying anachronism that had no place in modern life'. People had better amusements in cinemas, theatres, music halls and libraries, the *Guardian* declared. So it was goodbye to the fair.

Perhaps it was just as well fairs died off for they could be dangerous places. Aside from drink-fuelled brawls and pickpockets, the exhibits themselves could turn nasty. During the Elizabethan period, a lion at Loughborough fair escaped, fatally injuring a local townsman called Nicholas Wollands.

One-Offs
Many fairs and exhibits were once-in-a-lifetime specials, never to be repeated. In Leicestershire they included:

- An exhibition in 1830 for two months of Madame Tussaud's Waxworks at Leicester Theatre.
- A visit to Leicester by Buffalo Bill's Wild West Show in August 1891, billed as a 'Representation of Indian and Frontier Life', which featured genuine cowboys and Indians. The show set up camp on Belgrave Road's cricket and bicycle ground.
- In February 1784, in Leicester, the winter was so severe that the River Soar froze solid and a grand masquerade was held on the frozen water. Thousands of spectators gathered on the riverbanks and along the nearby West Bridge to watch a performance where 'Harlequin, Columbine, pantaloons and clown were represented.'

Leicestershire Wakes

Wakes were annual fairs held to commemorate the anniversary of the patron saint of the local church. A medieval custom, they reached the pinnacle of their popularity in Leicestershire during the early twentieth century.

The local gentry or employers often funded the wakes. At Bardon, the quarry owner laid on the August wake fair for the local schoolchildren. The streets were decorated and a band and parade opened the event, which culminated in a fair and tea on the village green.

But often wakes were not held at such pleasant times of the year because of the birthday of the church. Whetston and Ibstock's wakes occurred in October. Instead of bunting, the streets and fairground were lit with naphtha flares to illuminate the dark autumn days.

Festivals Today

Modern Leicestershire still keeps many of these old festivals alive, such as the traditional May celebrations held at places like Oadby, while Mayfest is a celebration of the month in general based at Stanford Hall, Lutterworth.

St George's Day celebrations have also been revived recently, especially in Leicester, which marks the occasion with parades and pageants across the city.

Leicester also commemorates its long history with events such as the Castle Park Festival and Riverside Festival. The city also hosts Dave's Comedy Festival, the longest running of its kind in Europe.

The county's Asian and Caribbean communities have further enriched Leicestershire's festival culture. Leicester's Caribbean Carnival, held every August since 1985, includes a spectacular procession of floats and musicians who parade through the city centre and Highfields district before culminating in a fair on Victoria Park.

In addition, the city celebrates the Chinese New Year, Holi, Dashera, the Sikh festival of Vaisakhi and the Jewish festival of Hanukkah. It is also the only UK city to mark the Hindu festival of Navratri. In 2016, Eid was marked with a mass celebration on Victoria Park when thousands of Muslims gathered to celebrate the end of Ramadan.

But one of Leicester's most famous festivals is Diwali – the celebration of the Hindu New Year. Diwali in Leicester is the biggest outside India, with over 30,000 people attending the celebrations. Festivities concentrate along the city's Golden Mile at Belgrave Road, extending into the city centre itself where Christmas lights are put up early to mark this festival of lights.

The Small and Large Screen

Bollywood in Leicestershire

Leicestershire in the twenty-first century has become a favourite location with Bollywood. In 2001 *Pyaar Ko Kya Naam Doon? (What Shall I Name This Love?)* became the first Bollywood film to be shot entirely on location in Leicester. Most of the sixty extras were locals. This was followed in 2004 by gangster film *Raakh (Ashes)*, which had 50 per cent of its scenes shot around the city.

Bollywood's interest has spread. In 2007, venues such as the University of Leicester's botanical gardens and the Grand Union Canal have featured in *Samunder Paar* (*Overseas*), an Indian TV series telling the story of British Asians.

In 2012, the Golden Mile became the city's latest star when it was used as a setting for the comedy *Jadoo*. Written by Leicester-born Amit Gupta, it is the story of two brothers, two restaurants and the ensuing war over the rights to their mother's recipe books. This time, the cast is probably more familiar to the general audience, featuring Madhur Jaffrey and actor Harish Patel of *Run Fatboy Run* fame.

Bollywood aside, Leicestershire is famous for its actors of the small and large screen …

Graham Chapman of Monty Python fame was born in Leicester, as was Parminder Nagra, who has starred in *Bend it Like Beckham*, *ER* and US crime drama *The Blacklist*. Michael Kitchen of *Foyles War* is also Leicestershire born, as is Richard Armitage, star of *Robin Hood*, *Spooks* and *The Hobbit* film trilogy.

Elsewhere in the county, Market Harborough has produced David Neilson, the actor who portrayed Roy Cropper on *Coronation Street*, and Una Stubbs was raised in Hinckley.

Music

Leicestershire is not short of famous musicians and bands. Kasabian originate from the county, with the band members hailing from Countisthorpe and Blaby. Other local musicians include Phil Oakley of the Human League, and David 'pick' Withers and John Illsley of Dire Straits. The '70s group Showaddywaddy, Mark Morrison of 'Return of the Mack' fame, Crazy Head and Frank Benbini of Fun Lovin' Criminals are also all Leicestershire born.

Local music festivals include Glastonbudget, the biggest tribute festival in Europe which is held at Turpost Farm, Wymeswold, and The Belgrave Mela which is a celebration of South Asian music and dance.

The Tourist Industry

The Home of the Package Tour

Thomas Cook was a cabinetmaker from Market Harborough. He was also a devoted member of the Leicester Temperance Society that he diligently walked to after work.

The Midlands County Railway seemed to Cook the perfect way to transport his Leicester brethren to a temperance rally at Southfields Park, Loughborough, so he contacted the railway to organise transport for a large party – a first in itself – before chartering the first privately hired excursion train offered to the general public.

On 5 July 1841, Cook packed 540 temperance campaigners into eight open-air third class carriages without seats! This was the first ever package tour. Each person paid 1 shilling for their rail fare, a brass band to entertain them, and tea and buns at their destination.

This early endeavour laid the foundation of Thomas Cook & Son. By 1850, Cook had offices along Leicester's Gallowtree Gate and was organising trips all over the world, including excursions to the Great Exhibition of 1851 and the first escorted trips for British travellers to the USA, the Middle East and Europe.

Spas

Leicestershire doesn't immediately spring to mind as a spa county, but the many sources of mineral-rich water have made it quite a spa hotspot – both in the past and today.

The Humberstone Gate Spa in Leicester was built in 1787 around a natural chalybeate spring in an attempt to make Leicester a spa town. However, the mineral content of the spring was too low and the venture folded.

The village of Shearsby was famous for the curative properties of its Holy Well that had long been credited with curing skin diseases, rheumatics, sickness and nervous disorders. So in the first half of the nineteenth century, the well was converted into a spa. But by 1855, the spa had fallen out of favour – probably because it was discovered that the main constitutes of the water were sodium sulphate and sodium chloride!

Ashby de la Zouch did successfully become a spa town and the chief town of north-west Leicestershire – before its success was supplanted by industrial Coalville.

But many spas in Leicestershire have flourished to this day. In the nineteenth century, Sapcote spa enjoyed lofty patronage. It was established in 1806 by John Frewen Turner who built a bathhouse over the so-called Golden Well along Stanton Road. The spa was equipped with cold and warm baths, and treatments for rheumatic and skin complaints.

The whole spa building cost £600 and was visited by the prime minister George Canning, and the Duke of Wellington.

Today, Leicestershire's star spa isn't centred around a water source but a former hunting lodge. Award-winning Ragdale Hall is set in the Leicestershire countryside. The spa doesn't have its own mineral-rich water source but it does have a unique, purpose-built thermal spa, which attracts not only visitors from the UK but as far afield as Dubai!

RELIGION AND SUPERSTITION

Leicestershire retains many traditions that preserve some of the old beliefs.

FOLK BELIEFS AND CUSTOMS

Beating the Bounds is an ancient custom that survived well into the nineteenth century. Every year (or every three years in the case of parishes such as St Mary's in Leicester) it was customary for the villagers to walk its parish boundaries, 'beating' them out with sticks. Young boys played a central role, with the boys themselves being hit at certain designated points.

Many experts believe this ritual corporal punishment was a weak survival of human sacrifice, offerings to the gods at set points along the borders and margins of a settlement to ensure they were well secured from threats.

According to John Nichols, each Easter around Shipley Hill near Cossington, 'lads and lasses of the adjacent villages meet upon Easter Monday yearly to make merry with cakes and ale.'

The locals regarded this custom to be an ancient tradition dating back to Celtic times. Another custom from the nearby Dane Hills was believed to be just as ancient. The hills were once wild countryside, reputedly haunted by the blue-faced hag, Black Annis, who was said to prey on local children.

Annis is probably a mis-rememberance of the Celtic goddess Anu or Danu, a goddess of fertility and the harvest. This probably explains the strange custom of the Easter Drag hunt, which was first recorded in 1668.

On the morning of each Easter Monday, races and contests were held on the Dane Hills. But at around noon, a dead cat soaked in aniseed was trailed in front of a pack of hounds just in front of Black Annis's bower and then dragged across the Leicester countryside with hounds, hunters and the mayor and his aldermen in hot pursuit. The hunt continued into Leicester itself, right up to the door of the mayor's house. Here the hunt ended in a formal dinner held by the mayor.

The hunts ceased in the eighteenth century, but local people continued to mark the occasion all the same and instead a fair was held on the Dane Hills – at least until the current housing estate was constructed!

May Day celebrations in Leicestershire underwent something of a renaissance in the nineteenth century, yet they retained the flavour of something older and pre-Christian.

Old songs show how it was common to begin the celebrations on May Eve, with parties going out to the woods at midnight, returning at dawn with branches and plants to weave into garlands. These garlands were placed at the front of village cottages for good luck.

Every village had its version of the May garland, which was based on a hoop lavishly decorated in flowers such as primrose, cowslip and a Leicestershire favourite, the marsh marigold. Some were single hoops, others double or triple and worked into a ball known as 'The May Bush'. Whatever the shape or form, inside each garland was at least one May doll.

The garlands were carried, covered in material (usually a lace curtain), in a procession through the villages, on sticks or on a flat basket. The participants sang songs and asked for gifts – a tame version of sacrifices. The May Bush – and its dolls – were only revealed to those who paid up – in food or money. No doubt the doll represented a spring goddess or ancient spirit of regeneration who would only bless those who sacrificed to her.

At harvest time, in Rempson, a local girl would be elected Queen of the Gleaners. On the first day of the harvest, the queen was crowned with wild flowers and corn and then carried in a chair to the first field to be cleared. It was for the queen to direct affairs, telling the villagers where to begin the gleaning and when to work. No one disobeyed the Queen of the Gleaners, for she undoubtedly represented a long-lost pagan goddess and to do so was to risk the harvest itself.

SACRED STONES

Leicestershire has no stone circles, but it does boast the odd standing stone or two. The Humberstone, which stood near Thurmaston, was a huge granite stone 'eight or perhaps ten feet' in height, and 6ft wide, according to *Gentleman's Magazine* – until the owner of the land it stood on decided it was in the way of his plough and so broke up the stone so that only a stump remained.

The stone, which gives its name to the nearby village of Humberstone, has been known variously as the Hoston, Hostin, Holy and Hell stone. The name Hel has been linked to the Norsemen as *Hel* was the name for the Norse underworld. The stone supposedly guarded a cave that was an entrance to the underworld – although no such place has been found.

But perhaps the stone did have some power, for the farmer who ordered its destruction went, in six years, from the owner of 120 acres to abject poverty, dying in the workhouse.

Another stone with a similar reputation was St John's Stone, which stood on farmland near Leicester Abbey. Local children used to visit the stone each 24 June – Midsummer's Eve. They would dance around the 7ft high, 3ft wide monolith, but ensured they left well before dark to avoid the wrath of the fairies. In 1840, like the Humberstone, St John's Stone was completely destroyed.

HOLY WELLS

Sketchley Well was famous as a brightener of intellects. Anyone who was stupid or dull witted was often advised to 'go to Sketchley' to take the waters while someone who came out with a sudden witticism was remarked as having 'been to Sketchley'.

The well at Bruntingthorpe went from holy to hotel. It was situated just outside the village, where a spring spouted into a round pit.

The taste of the spring was described as salty and brackish and useless as a drinking source, even for cattle, but when a local boy with a scorbutic ailment bathed in it and was cured, it was converted into a spa in the nineteenth century and today is the location of the Shearsby Bath Hotel.

CHURCHES

Fleckney Church and the Fairies
Local superstitions also play their part in the founding of many of Leicestershire's churches. The fairy folk were believed to

have had a hand in the location of Fleckney church. When the foundation stones of the church were originally laid at a site a mile outside of the present village, each night the disgruntled supernatural residents dismantled them and threw them in a nearby stream.

The waters of the stream carried the stones for a distance until they became lodged. Eventually, the builders became resigned to circumstance and decided to build where the material came to rest. Obviously this was well away from the fairies domain as the church was this time allowed to stand.

St Nicholas Church: The Oldest Church in Leicester

St Nicholas church in Leicester is located at what was the heart of Roman Leicester – right next door to the Jewry Wall Museum.

Built in AD 880, it is Leicester's oldest standing place of worship. It was also the city's first cathedral – before the Anglo-Saxon bishopric of Leicester passed to Lincoln in the eleventh century. Originally, the church was built from masonry scavenged from the abandoned Roman baths next door. Later, the Normans embellished it, and later still the niche in the canopy of the north aisle was added – a remnant from William Wyggeston's original hospital.

The church is a survivor, withstanding Viking attacks and the brutal redevelopment of Leicester in the 1960s when much of the city's medieval past was destroyed. Only St Nicholas remains in the area, a sole survivor marooned in an island in the middle of the city's ring road.

The Church that Died of Shame

St Mary in Arden in Market Harborough had a bad reputation. Its churchmen were disreputable and the church itself was a bastion of clandestine marriages.

Eventually, in 1650, its privileges were annulled. The church felt the shame of this fall from grace so keenly that reputedly its tower followed suit, crashing down and destroying the main body of the church.

Frisby on the Wreak: The Gretna Green of the Midlands

The Church of St Thomas of Canterbury in Frisby on the Wreake had a similar reputation to St Mary's, although it seems to have managed to remain intact. Between 1756 and 1796, the Revd William Brecknock Wragg was its vicar. The Revd Wragg happily did away with the banns and married any couple on demand, making it a quick stop point for couples eager to be wed. He even married one couple in the parlour of the village inn!

Weddings during the reverend's tenure went up from three or four a year to ten a year. The parish records indicate a large portion of the marriages were between persons from distant parishes who were clearly marrying at Frisby because of the relaxed rules.

However, the law caught up with the obliging vicar when he was tried and sentenced to fourteen years' transportation – a sentence that was set aside because of his advancing old age. So he was defrocked instead.

Beeby Tub

> *Beeby tub was to have been a spire*
> *Two brothers fought and broke their necks and so 'twas built no higher.*

The stubby spire – and unusual name – of the church at the village of Beeby is explained by a sad tale. Two brothers were engaged by the Abbot of Leicester to build a church at nearby Queniborough. The spire was magnificent, visible for miles around and the Abbot of Croyland and owner of the Manor of Beeby was jealous. He decided his church must be similarly endowed. So he asked for the names of the two masons.

But whereas the build at Queniborough went off without a hitch, work at Beeby was anything but harmonious. The brothers could not agree on the design, and money for the build was short, adding to the tension.

Eventually the tower was built – all but for the spire. And the brothers again began to argue – on top of the church – about whether the tower would take the spire's weight. Words turned to blows and such was the ferocity of the fight that they plunged to the ground – onto the very stones that were to build the disputed spire.

To this day, the tower remains incomplete – with only a stub instead of a spire.

The Abbey of St Mary in the Fields

The Abbey of St Mary in the Fields, known as Leicester Abbey, was founded in 1143 by the second Earl of Leicester, Robert le Bossu. It was the wealthiest religious establishment in Leicestershire, as well as one of the largest Augustinian abbeys in England and the place of death of the unfortunate Cardinal Wolsey.

The abbey survived until 1538, largely due to its final abbot, Bourchier, who was installed by Cromwell to ensure a smooth dissolution. Nonetheless, Bourchier did his best to save the abbey, persuading its canons to accept the king as head of the Church of England, and making gifts to Cromwell. But it was all in vain, and on 28 August 1538 it was finally surrendered.

Twycross Church

Twycross church's thirteenth-century eastern window is thought to be the oldest stained-glass window in England. However, it didn't originate in Leicestershire. Instead, it reached its final destination by a rather convoluted route.

The window originated in the Saint Chapelle, Paris, from where it was transported during the French Revolution for safe-keeping in England. But it never made it. Instead, it was presented as a gift to George III, inherited by William IV, who in turn passed it on to Lord Howe, who installed it in Twycross.

The Smallest Church in Leicestershire

Snibston is home to thirteenth-century St Mary's church, the smallest church in England that is still in use. Despite having the capacity for only thirty worshippers, regular weekly worship still occurs there.

Mount St Bernard Abbey

Founded in 1835, Mount St Bernard Abbey near Coalville is the first permanent monastery founded in England since the Reformation. Dedicated to the Cistercian order, it is also the only Trappist monastery in England.

Its original monks fled France after the French revolutions of the late eighteenth century and the 1830s. Their intended destination was Canada but after a brief stopover in Ireland, they eventually found their way to north-west Leicestershire.

The monks initially lived in a four-room cottage until the monastery, designed by Augustus Pugin, was completed in 1844.

Mount St Bernard has played host to a variety of famous visitors: William Wordsworth visited in 1841 and other visitors included Florence Nightingale and the Pre-Raphaelite Edward Burne Jones, who wrote in his later years how 'More and more my heart is pining for that monastery in the Charnwood Forest. Why there? I don't know, only that I saw it when I was little and have hankered after it ever since.'

The monks farmed the land about the abbey but also did a great deal to alleviate the poverty of the local people. The great Irish famine led to a major influx of Irish immigrants to the area. In 1845, Mount St Bernard gave refuge to 2,788 people while another 18,887 were given food.

In 1847, a further '36,000 people received charity and hospitality from the hands of the monks' according to the *Catholic Institute Magazine*. In the 1850s, a reformatory for young Catholic delinquents was also established. This charity work continued after the Leicestershire coalfield suffered a depression in the 1870s and also during the General Strike of 1926.

In 2009, the abbey was used as the site for the re-interment of 600 medieval Trappist monks exhumed from the former site of Stratford Langthorne Abbey in London that was excavated as part of the extension of the Jubilee line.

Mount St Bernard was proposed as a temporary resting site for the bones of Richard III before his reburial in Leicester

Cathedral but the University of Leicester refused to release the bones.

SAINTS, MARTYRS, DISSENTERS AND HERETICS

Early Christian Martyrs in Leicester?

Leicestershire may be able to date its Christianity to pagan times, if Andrew Breeze, a lecturer at the University of Navarre in Spain, is correct. Breeze believes that two early Christian martyrs, killed in Roman Britain sometime in the third century AD, could have met their deaths in Leicester.

The men are two of three Christians recorded by the Venerable Bede as being put to death in Roman Britain. The two men – Aaron and Julius – apparently died at 'the city of the legions'. Many historians believe this to refer to Caerleon in Wales, but Dr Breeze, referring to the writings of Gildas, says the monks' writings point out the martyrs were buried in lands under Anglo-Saxon rule – ruling out the Welsh city. The only other choice for the city of the legions is Leicester.

St Wistan

The ninth-century heir to the Kingdom of Mercia, Wistan, was a pious young man more interested in the religious life than the throne. However, Wistan's cousin, Brifardus, was keen to be king and so plotted his cousin's murder.

Brifardus invited Wistan to an assembly on 1 June near the River Sence in Leicestershire, close to the village of Wigston. Here, he struck down Wistan with the hilt of his sword, after which one of his men stabbed the king in the back.

Wistan's corpse was buried at Repton in Derbyshire, then capital of Mercia. But the site of his murder developed a reputation for strange sights and miracles. A column of light was seen ascending to heaven and every year on 1 June, human hair was said to sprout from the ground at the spot where Wistan's head hit the ground.

These miraculous occurrences convinced people of Wistan's sainthood and drove Brifardus mad. Meanwhile, a shrine and a church were built near the site of the saint's death, and a village grew up which became known as Wistanstowe – the holy place of Wistan – later shortened to Wistow.

Wistow became a place of pilgrimage, and in 1167 the Archbishop of Canterbury himself made a pilgrimage there. He, the Abbot of Leicester and other notables all witnessed the hairy growth from the martyr's murder site, which they observed disappeared within the hour.

Hugh Latimer

Although not a Catholic saint, Hugh Latimer was one of the three Oxford martyrs of Anglicanism.

Born at Thurcaston in the late fifteenth century, Latimer studied at Cambridge and was ordained as a priest around 1510. He was one of the earliest Protestant reformers and gained royal favour by supporting Henry VIII's efforts to annul his first marriage to Catherine of Aragon.

Thus his rise to power began. Latimer became Bishop of Worcester and chaplain to the boy king Edward VI.

But it all went wrong when Edward's Catholic sister, Mary, ascended the throne. In 1553 Latimer was arrested on charges of treason. He was tried in oxford and burned at the stake on 16 October 1555.

The Lollards

The term *Lollard* comes from the Dutch for a murmurer or babbler of prayers. But it acquired a more dangerous meaning in medieval England, being applied to heretics who rejected much of the pomp of the high church, disdaining adornments, money and unnecessary ceremony in religion.

Leicestershire seemed to have a particular affinity with this dissenting religion and was an early centre for its nurture. The Earl of Leicestershire, John of Gaunt, allowed practicing Lollard clerics such as John Wycliffe to exist under his protection. Wycliffe was installed as rector of Lutterworth parish church between 1374 and 1384 and it was while there that he first translated the bible into English.

Meanwhile, ordinary people were also taking the lead. A certain William, a smith of Leicester, was one noted case. Self-educated, Smith became a Lollard, abstaining from meat and alcohol. He held meetings at the chapel of St John the Baptist in Leicester where he set up his headquarters.

Smyth garnered considerable support in the town, probably because he advocated that the people should have the right to hold to account lords and clergy who were 'evildoers'. He also maintained that collective prayer was useless, as was paying for prayers; good living was sufficient. This essentially was the same as saying the clergy was redundant.

Henry of Knighton records that in the event of running out of firewood for cooking at his headquarters, Smyth and a companion took an old wooden image of St Catherine from the chapel and used it for firewood, joking that they were martyring the saint for a second time.

At the end of October 1389, the Archbishop of Canterbury, William Courtney, arrived at Leicester Abbey to deal with the Lollard problem. He called William Smyth and seven others to an ecclesiastic court to answer the charge of Lollardy. The men absconded and so were excommunicated in their absence. But as the Lollards were being shielded by the sympathetic folk of

Leicester, Courtney placed the whole town under an interdict. Until the fugitives were betrayed or gave themselves up, no church services would be held and the sacraments would be denied the dying.

But Lollardy continued and not just in Leicester. In the fifteenth century, a William Trivet of Twyford was convicted of being a Lollard and whipped seven times around St Martin's church in Leicester and once around the market place.

The Burning of Thomas Moore

The reign of Mary I was a dangerous time for those of a reforming nature after the queen tried to zealously re-establish Catholicism across the country.

In April 1556, 24-year-old Thomas Moore was visiting a church in Leicester with some friends. During the visit, Moore was unwise enough to voice some of his more reforming religious opinions, remarking that the statues of the saints were mere empty idols, as was the Eucharist.

An eavesdropper duly reported Thomas and he was summoned to appear in St Margaret's church before the Bishop of Lincoln, Dr John White. At this trial, the bishop tested him. He placed a pyx – a box containing the sacramental wafer – on the altar of the church and asked Thomas what he saw before him. Thomas replied that he saw only ornaments. The bishop then asked if the 'blood, flesh and bones' of Christ were not in the little box?

Moore replied no and thus doomed himself. He was found guilty of heresy. He refused to recant his beliefs and so on 26 June 1556 he was burnt at the stake.

George Fox and the Quakers

In 1667, the Society of Friends or Quakers took on the form we recognise today due to the beliefs and efforts of George Fox, a weaver's son from Fenny Drayton.

Fox was a serious young man, who disdained luxury and indulgence. For years, he pondered the religious question that troubled him and after a lengthy study of the bible, he began to formulate his own religious beliefs. Fox rejected ritual and group prayer, believing salvation lay in a person's heart. He disdained church worship, believing god should be communed with in the open air and even held the view that women and children could minister.

In 1647, Fox began preaching. One of his first addresses was at Sutton in the Elms outside the parish church. It was at this point that he began to gather a group of like-minded individuals of 'friends' who formed the beginnings of the Quakers.

A local story tells how in 1662, Fox and some friends were arrested at Swannington and committed to Leicester gaol. There they continued to hold their prayer meetings – until the gaoler tried to break them up by setting his mastiff on them. But the dog was better disposed towards the Quakers and instead, when its master raised his staff to strike the prisoners, the dog seized it and ran off to play.

John Wesley

The founder of Methodism was a frequent visitor to Leicestershire. On 31 July 1770, he lodged at a house in St Nicholas Street as he planned a series of sermons in the town.

Described as a short man, with long white hair and black clothing, Wesley's speech, in the yard of Leicester Castle, was initially rained off and postponed until 5 a.m. the following morning at a house on Millstone Lane, which was a common meeting place for his followers.

Markfield has close links with the Methodist movement and according to a blue plaque on the church, its founder John Wesley paid thirteen visits. He was allowed to preach in the parish church but his visits became so popular that he had to accommodate larger crowds by preaching on the village green.

WITCHCRAFT

The belief in witchcraft continued widely in Leicestershire up until relatively recently. According to an Elmesthorpe farmer in 1811:

> It is common almost everywhere amongst the women that when they brew they make crosses to keep the witch out of the mash-tub, so that the ale might be fine … farmers and common folk were very great believers in old popular tales of ghost, fairies and witches and of people and cattle being under the evil tongue.

Cases of witchcraft in Leicestershire can be traced back to the Middle Ages. In 1326, a Robert le Mareschal was charged and hanged for the crime of attempting to kill Edward II by witchcraft.

Even the clergy were suspect. On 3 December 1440, Bishop Almwich arrived at Leicester to investigate accusations of sorcery against Abbot Sadyngton of Leicester Abbey. The abbott was investigating a sum of stolen money and when no one confessed, he turned to sorcery. His accusers stated he had taken a young boy to Ingarsby Grange and after murmuring incantations, anointed his thumbnail and bid the boy scry to find the culprit. As a result a Thomas Ashby, the cathedral canon, was accused of the theft.

The abbot was disliked by his brethren, which probably accounts for the accusation. Perhaps this was why the bishop was lenient and simply allowed Abbot Sadyngton to purge himself of the crime.

But it was after the Reformation that Leicestershire's major witch trials began.

James I and the Witches of Leicester

In 1603, James VI of Scotland ascended the English throne to become James I of England. James had an interest in witchcraft. His ideas seem to have infected his subjects because a series of trials began across the country.

A case that James himself took an interest in and could be said to have solved was that of the bewitching of 12-year-old John Smythe of Husbands Bosworth in 1616. John claimed to be in the thrall of a group of witches who possessed him with their animal familiars. Nine women were arrested and in July 1616 put on trial.

The women were tried over several days, with John appearing in court to offer the judges first-hand evidence of the 'strange fits' brought about by their magic. Robert Herrick described the evidence to his brother Sir William in a letter:

Sir Henry Gastings hath done what he could to hold him in his fit but he and another as strong as he could not hold him.' Said Hastings, 'If he [John] might have his arm at liberty, he would strike himself such blows on his breast ... that you might hear the sound of it the length of the chamber ... and yet all he did to himself did him no hurt ... 6 of the witches had 6 several spirits-one in the likeness of a horse, another a dog, another a cat, another a fullemer, another a fish, another a cock with whom everyone of them tormented him ... when the horse tormented him he would whinny, when the cat tormented him he would cry like a cat. When he was in his fit, they would sometimes [be] brought to him and then they were charged to speak certain words and to name their spirits and one of them speak to another as thus.

The women were found guilty and hanged. But some months later, the king himself was in Leicester and, intrigued by the case, took the opportunity to question John Smythe about his unpleasant experience. The boy, perhaps awed by the king, crumbled and admitted he had made the whole story up.

The Witches of Belvoir Castle
A few years later, in 1618, the sixth Earl of Rutland, Francis Manners, lord of Belvoir Castle and friend to the king, was himself troubled by witchcraft.

Francis was unlucky with his wives and children. His first wife died in 1608 and after his remarriage, his son and heir Henry died, quickly followed by his second son Francis.

Both the earl and his second wife believed the deaths to be caused by witchcraft. They laid the crime firmly at the door of three former servants: Joan Flowers and her daughters Philippa and Margaret. Their masters had become dissatisfied with their work and their opinion of them became very low. Philippa was described as 'lewdly transported with the love of one Thomas Simpson' and Joan described as 'a monstrous, malicious woman, full of oaths, curses and imprecations, irreligious and for anything they saw by her, a plain atheist.'

All three were sacked, with Margaret the only one offered a pay-off of 40 shillings, a pillow and a mattress of wool. Joan, angry at her treatment, was said to have placed a curse on her former employers. Soon afterwards, the earl and countess became ill with vomiting and convulsions and Henry and Francis died.

The earl ordered the women's arrest and they were taken to Lincoln for questioning, where Joan was accused of murder and her daughters of being accomplices. To prove her innocence, Joan asked for bread and butter, saying if she was guilty 'let it never pass through her'. Minutes after biting into the bread, she died.

Philippa and Margaret admitted to witchcraft. According to their testimony, they had communed with spirits through their familiar, a cat called Rutterkin. Margaret described how Henry was killed. She had stolen one of Henry's gloves and passed it to Joan, who stroked Rutterkin with it before dipping it in hot water and pricking it. To prevent any further heirs, they stole feathers from the earl's bed and a pair of gloves, which they boiled in water and blood.

In the course of the investigation, the Flowers also implicated Anne Baker of Bottesford, Joan Willimot of Goodby and Ellen Greene of Stathorne as witches who helped them in their vendetta against the earl.

Although no action was taken against these three women, Margaret and Philippa were convicted by their own words and hanged. It is likely that Joan was throttled rather than chocking on a condemning bit of bread. Philippa and Margaret were probably tortured into their confessions – or may even have been offered leniency. Either way, justice was seen to be done.

The Last Incitement for Witchcraft

A hundred years later, Leicestershire was the last recorded place in the UK where an accused witch was 'swum' and indicted for witchcraft in a secular court.

On 4 August 1717, twenty-five people stood at Leicester Assizes to bear witness against Jane Clarke of Wigston Magna and her son and daughter Joseph and Mary, who were charged with cursing members of the village.

The trio were specifically charged with bewitching a Mary Hatchings to death while tormenting others with illness by 'twisting and distorting of their limbs backwards and forwards' and appearing to their victims at night 'in their own and other shapes'.

A church minister was unable to help the victims so a local cunning man was called in who identified a curse. The urine of the victims was sealed in a bottle and then heated in fire. If the urine remained in the bottle, all was well but if it came out, the afflicted remained cursed. When the urine was set to boil, the witches supposedly came into the room, as a cat or a dog or as themselves. They sat on the chimney racks shaking their fists at the bewitched and grinning in a threatening manner before vanishing up the chimney.

The cunning man completed the cure with a balm of rosemary and marigold in boiled ale and blood was rubbed onto their chests. The blood was that of the victim – but also the witches too.

To acquire the blood, the villagers pursued the Clarkes and bled them. But they also decided to take the opportunity to acquire evidence for the authorities – using tried and tested measures. Firstly, the witches were 'swum':

> 'Their thumbs and great toes tyed fast together and were thrown so bound into the water' where 'tho they strove and used all endeavours to sink yet they all swam like acorke or an empty barrel.'

Evidently all three floated because they were brought before the assizes. Other evidence presented to the court included bits of stone, dirt and thatch reportedly voided from the victim's bodies. Mary Hatchings also had teeth marks, some human some dog-like, which were attributed to Mary and Joseph rather than their elderly mother.

But even though the common people still believed in witchcraft, the authorities did not and there were no more witch trials in Leicester.

The Witch of Aston

Yet the accusations still came. In July 1776, an old woman of 80 from Aston was accused of bewitching a woman in neighbouring Earl Shilton. According to the *Leicester and Nottingham Chronicle*, the victim had suffered for some years from a mark resembling the bite of a tarantula.

On 20 July, the woman's husband and her solider son set upon the old lady, threatening her and held her at sword point, demanding blood from her body and a blessing to remove the curse. The old lady complied but the 'cure' didn't work.

On 24 July, local vigilantes, raised by the family and pretending to have a warrant, threw the old lady into a horse pond 'with uncommon brutality' but fortunately she escaped with her life, despite sinking. In fact, it was the mob that was at risk of indictment as the paper called for the local magistrates to 'exert themselves to bring to punishment these atrocious offenders'.

Witches of Leicester and the Highcross

Today, Leicestershire's witches are the winners. In 2007, the *Telegraph* reported that a local coven was protesting about the name of Leicester's new shopping complex. The proposed name was the Highcross Quarter – to commemorate Leicester's old high cross. But the witches felt this was a misuse of a term used for festivals of the Wiccan calendar.

Rather than use magic, the witches turned to the power of the Internet, staking their claim to the name through domain names. But maybe stranger powers were afoot. After trying to buy up the names, and then threatening to take the witches to the United Nations World Intellectual Property Organization, the developers inexplicably dropped their claim, opting for the name 'High Cross' instead.

RELIGION TODAY

Today, Leicestershire's religious composition is the most diverse it has ever been – largely because of the make-up of the population of the city of Leicester. The 2011 census shows that while 32.40 per cent of people in the city were nominally Christian, 22.82 per cent had no religion, 18.63 per cent were Muslim, a further 15.19 per cent were Hindu, 4.38 per cent Sikh, 0.56 other, 0.37 per cent Buddhist, and 0.09 per cent Jewish. And in 5.56 per cent religion was not stated.

Leicester is the only city in the UK to significantly mark the Hindu festival of Navratri and is the home of the UK's first Hindu temple in 1969. The city is also the site of the first Jain temple in the Western world. A Hindu sect, the Jains established themselves in Leicester in 1983 by converting a former Victorian congregational chapel. Marble and stone were laid over the plain Victorian brickwork to create a façade of gods and goddesses.

INVASION, CONQUEST, WAR AND REBELLION

ROMANS, BRITONS, SAXONS, VIKINGS

Boudica's Defeat

No one really knows where the iconic queen Boudica made her last stand against the Roman invaders, but one possible site lies in Leicestershire. Kevin K. Carroll has suggested that the junction between Watling Street and Fosse at High Cross is a likely contender as it would have been the perfect spot for the second legion Augusta to move up from Exeter to join the rest of Suetonius's forces at the final, decisive battle for ancient Britain.

Aethelfleda the Liberator

In AD 868, the Vikings invaded Leicestershire, part of a concerted Norse/Danish campaign to capture England. Viking longships swarmed down the River Soar, with the city of Leicester in their sights.

They conquered Leicester, destroying some of its old Roman defences, while the rest of the Leicestershire countryside was being dealt with in typical Viking style, with sites like Breedon Monastery pillaged and destroyed.

By AD 874, Mercia, of which Leicestershire was just a small part, was firmly in Norse hands. The war of conquest was not yet

over but a stalemate had been reached. In AD 886, in an attempt
to prevent further bloodshed, the extent of Danish territory was
agreed by a treaty between Alfred the Great and Guthrum, King
of the Danes. Known as the Danelaw, it made Mercia – and by
default Leicestershire – a Scandinavian county of England – at
least for a while.

But Alfred's daughter, Aethelfleda, had no truck with the treaty.
In AD 911, she was Lady of Mercia in her own right after the
death of her husband, Aethelred. So she made it her mission to
rid Mercia of the Danes. In AD 918, she liberated Leicester, the
sheer strength of her forces and her reputation causing the Danish
invaders to quit and relinquish the town.

To ensure security, Aethelfleda refortified Leicester and
reputedly built its first castle.

MEDIEVAL MADNESS

The Norman Conquest

After the Battle of Hastings in 1066, the Norman consolidation of power across England didn't go quite as smoothly as they had hoped. In Leicestershire, a descendant of one of the county's previous Danish interlopers was responsible for the resistance to the new invaders.

Eric the Forester was a descendant of a Danish chief called Ericke, who had invaded England at the time of King Alfred. Eric was a great landowner – and he wasn't about to relinquish any power to the Norman invaders. So he raised an army from his own estates in Leicestershire and made a last stand.

He held off the Norman forces at Copt Oak near Ulverscroft for some time but was ultimately defeated and lost his lands anyway. But William the Conqueror so admired his efforts that his life was spared. He was given special office, commanding the forces of William, and eventually allowed to retire to his own house in Leicestershire.

Reputedly, the Herrick family are his descendants.

Anarchy in the UK

In the twelfth century, Princess Matilda, despite being declared the heir of her father Henry I, had lost support of the English barons and so in 1135 when he died, they shifted their allegiance to the king's nephew, Stephen.

With the support of her half-brother, the Earl of Gloucester, Matilda began a bitter war for the crown with Stephen. So began a nineteen-year period of English history known as The Anarchy, when England fought against itself.

Leicestershire's earl, Robert de Beaumont, was a close adviser of the new king and so Leicestershire no doubt was a target for the enraged queen's forces. The earl fortified Shilton Hill and a new motte and bailey castle at Kirby was constructed to defend the main roads crossing the county.

But it was at Leicester Castle that peace was effectively made. The barons of both armies began to meet in secret to make private treaties that would force Stephen and Matilda and her son Henry to come to terms. Robert Beaumont was chief amongst the earls who led the peace movement, a movement that culminated in the Treaty of Wallingford that was sealed in Westminster in December 1153, making Henry Stephen's heir.

The Razing of Leicester

However, Robert's son, Robert Blanchemain, third Earl of Leicestershire, was not so supportive of the new king – an action that was to have dire consequences for him and Leicestershire.

In 1173, Robert sided with the king's rebellious wife, Eleanor, and her sons. The rebellion did not work out well. At the Battle of Bury St Edmunds, Robert was taken prisoner. The king's forces entered Leicestershire to seize Blanchemain's lands. Earl Shilton Castle was destroyed. But worse still lay ahead for Leicester.

On 28 July, the siege of Leicester began. The Norman forces in the castle forced the Saxon townsfolk to hold off the king's forces, but eventually they broke through and showed no mercy to the beleaguered townsfolk.

According to Throsby's history, Leicester was:

> … fired in several places at once and what the flames could not destroy was thrown down by force of men and engines. The Roman walls were pulled down and the town laid waste to: dismantled to wear the badge of its owners disobedience and treason.

Meanwhile, Leicester Castle continued to hold out but was eventually forced to yield. When it did, Leicester's punishment was completed. Now the punishment of the townsfolk was completed. Some were fined but others were banished.

The War of the Roses

On 22 August 1485, the forces of Richard III finally met with those of Henry Tudor at Market Bosworth.

The king had spent his penultimate night in Leicester's Blue Boar Inn before riding out for what was to be his final battle – and the final battle of any anointed British monarch on English soil.

Richard had the dominant army – until the troops of Sir William Stanley, who had sworn allegiance to Richard but was Henry Tudor's stepfather, deserted the king.

According to local accounts, villagers at Stoke Golding climbed the battlements of St Margaret of Antioch church to watch the battle. Grooves in the windowsills of the church are attributed to soldiers sharpening their swords there on the battle's eve.

But Stoke Golding was also to play another part in the end of the War of the Roses – and the beginning of the new regime, for the village played host to the crowning of the new king and the 'birthplace of the Tudor dynasty'. After the battle, Henry and his entourage retired to the hilly country near the village. The coronation was performed with a circlet (Richard's crown?) retrieved from a thorn bush – in the area known as Crown Hill and Crown Hill Field.

In the meantime, large pits were dug around the villages and neighbouring Dadlington and Fenny Drayton, where the battle's dead were buried. Richard himself was returned to Leicester and an ignominious display and burial.

Debates still continue about the exact location of the battlefield. Ambion Hill was the favoured location and site of the battlefield heritage centre, due to a sentence in the chronicles of Raphael Holinshed who wrote in 1577 that Richard, the night before the battle, 'pitched his field on a hill called Anne Beame, refreshed his soldiers and took his rest'. This was interpreted to mean that Ambion Hill was the battlefield site. But there were other local contenders.

Between 2005 and 2009, a large-scale project by Glenn Foard of the Battlefield Trust attempted to identify a definitive location. It is now accepted that the core area of the battle occurred around Fenn Lanes, 2 miles south-west of the visitor centre. The decisive evidence was a concentration of cannonball and gun shot, remains of an ancient marsh and a small silver gilt badge shaped like a boar, the emblem of Richard III, which was given out to his followers.

Ambion Hill, however, still remains part of the wider battlefield.

REFORMATION RISINGS

The advent of the Tudor dynasty did no more to ensure peace in Leicestershire than any of the previous regimes. All was quiet through the reign of Henry VIII but with his death, and the death of his most immediate heir the boy king Edward, disruption once again broke out.

Leicestershire was central to much of this, not least because Lady Jane Grey, the nine days queen who briefly supplanted the rightful Queen Mary, was a local girl.

Leicestershire may have declared allegiance to Mary instead, but that did not stop the county harbouring pockets of unrest.

Wyatt's Rebellion
Learning no lessons from his daughter's historically short reign and imprisonment at the hands of her disgruntled cousin, Jane's father, Henry Grey, first Duke of Suffolk, decided to have another pop at his rightful monarch, along with his brother Thomas, the Earl of Devon, and various other peeved peers.

The lords of the rebellion, known as Wyatt's Rebellion, were supposed to raise support from their counties before converging on London and again replacing the queen – this time with her sister Elizabeth. However, the rebellion was thwarted when the Crown got wind of it.

Some of the would-be rebels had the sense to withdraw but Henry Grey was determined to press on – but he only managed to raise 140 men. He gave himself up but was tried and beheaded, with his daughter and his son-in-law following him. The irony is, if Grey had not revolted, Jane would probably have lived, as Mary knew well she was only a pawn. Wyatt's Rebellion, however, convinced her that she could remain a nucleus for dissent – unless she was moved from the board of play.

Meanwhile, Leicester itself was the scene of local repercussions when John Kettle, who seems to have been part of the rebellion, was hung, drawn and quartered in the town on 9 March 1554 – the only case of this in the town's history.

Kettle's remains – according to the town accounts – were displayed about the town: his head fitted to the High Cross and his four quarters over the town gates.

May Day and Puritans

On 1 May 1603, the town of Leicester erupted into violence when its puritan overlords attempted to suppress the traditional May Day revels.

Henry Hastings, the Earl of Huntingdon, was overlord of Leicester and a zealous puritan who was trying to convert the townsfolk to his beliefs by allowing equally enthusiastic preachers to lecture them on the error of their ways.

It did little good. The Mayor of Leicester grumbled that despite prohibition, townsfolk had been stealing wood from Sir Henry for the idolatrous purpose of making maypoles.

So the authorities moved in to suppress the celebrations. But the town stewards met staunch opposition and a riot ensued. The people of Leicester roamed the streets, many armed with guns, seeking out the puritan killjoys. Things didn't settle down for another two weeks.

The Midland Revolt

The Midland Revolt was a series of riots that arose in the Midlands as a protest against the enclosure of common land. It was led by a tinker called John Reynolds, otherwise known as Captain Pouch (because of the fact he promised his supporters by 'the contents of his pouch' that they would suffer no harm by defying the authorities).

The intention of the revolt was to destroy the enclosures but Pouch urged his followers to use no violence in their endeavours. Instead, the idea was to tear down the hedges and fences enclosing the land.

The revolt began in the spring of 1607 in Northamptonshire and by May had spread to Leicestershire. Five thousand people massed at Cotesbach in Leicestershire, where the owner of the land, John Quarles, had raised rents for his tenant farmers – no doubt to drive them out so he could add their farms to the other parcels of land that he had already begun to enclose for sheep farming.

To stem the flow of supporters for the Cotesbach protest, a curfew was imposed upon Leicester and a gibbet raised to warn the people of the consequences of the riot. It did little good, as the townsfolk tore it down.

But the revolt was also as ineffectual, for by 1612 the enclosure of land was complete and never repealed.

The English Civil War

With very few exceptions, Leicestershire was firmly on the side of Parliament during the English Civil War. Although Viscount Falkland of Shilton Park, Tooley, backed the king (and died for it), other great families were against the Crown.

Unsurprisingly, the Greys of Groby took the side of the rebels – probably because of their past tussles with the Crown. But the clergy was also on the side of Parliament and often became targets for vengeful Crown loyalists. In March 1644, Colonel Hastings of Ashby de la Zouch led four troops of horses around the county, arresting 100 clergymen and their supporters. They were held at Hinckley church.

The city of Leicester was firmly in Parliament's camp and on 30 May 1645, Royalist forces held the city under siege, only breaching the walls in the early hours of the morning.

Their retribution on the town was merciless. While defenders on the town's rooftops attempted to drive them off with shot and roof tiles, the Royalist forces drove the defenders further into the centre of Leicester until at High Cross and St Martin's churchyard they made a last stand. Here, they finally laid down their weapons – only to be charged by the Royalist cavalry.

At the trial of Charles I, it was claimed the king himself egged his troops on. One Humphrey Brown testified that Charles was heard to say, 'I do not care if they are cut, they are mine enemies.'

Whether Charles gave the order or not, the Royalist repercussions were bloody. Women and children were dragged from their homes and killed and the members of the town committee hanged or dismembered. By the end of the siege, 709 people were estimated dead.

A month later in June 1645, Harborough became the headquarters of the king's army. It was in the town that Charles I decided to confront parliamentary forces at nearby Naseby, just over the border in Northamptonshire. The Battle of Naseby proved a decisive victory for Parliament led by Oliver Cromwell and, after the battle, Harborough chapel became a temporary prison for the captured forces.

Following the battle, parliamentary forces pursued defeated Royalists over the border into Leicester to Great Glen. Here the church was vandalised during the ensuing skirmish and still bears the scars today. Modern Great Glen preserves its memories of the episode in five road names: Cromwell Road, Naseby Way, Rupert's Way, Edgehill Close and Halford Close.

Both sides were guilty of putting the people of Leicestershire to great hardship through looting. In 1642, parliamentary troops stole horses and provisions from villages near Ashby Parva, while in 1646, the citizens of Dadlington lodged a complaint with the Warwickshire county committee that on 12 March 1643, a parliamentary solider called Burdett had made off with a horse belonging to a local widow.

TWENTIETH-CENTURY CONFLICT

The First World War

Zeppelins Over Loughborough

On 31 January 1916, nine Zeppelin airships set out to bomb Liverpool docks. They missed their target because of fog, but as blackouts at this time were not mandatory – especially in many country towns – it was easy for the airships to spot the lights of Loughborough, and the commander, Captain Franz Stabert, gave the order to drop the bombs over the town instead.

Bombs landed in Ashby Square, The Rushes and Thomas Street respectively, with the fourth and final bomb killing five people on Empress Road. The airship went on to drop bombs on Ilkeston and Burton upon Trent.

The Great Donington Escape

During the war, Donington Hall in Castle Donington served as a prisoner-of-war camp with two 6ft-high electric barbed-wire fences and an electric wire erected around its perimeter.

Yet despite these precautions, in May 1915 Gunther Plüschow successfully escaped not only Donington but Britain – the only German POW to do so in two world wars. Plüschow recalls in his memoirs:

> Day and night I planned, brooded, deliberated how I could escape from this miserable imprisonment. I had to act with the greatest calm and caution if I hoped to succeed.

After quizzing a guard and discovering the nearest train station was at Derby, Plüschow obtained civilian clothes and hid with another inmate while another prisoner deceived the nightly roll call. At 12.30 a.m., using a ladder and planks to scale the fence, the two men escaped.

Making their way cross-country to Derby, they split up and made for London via Leicester. Although his companion was recaptured, Plüschow's English was better and helped him convince people he was an American seaman. An attempt was even made to recruit him to the British Army!

At Gravesend, he stole a rowing boat and stowed away on the SS *Princess Juliana* and so reached Europe, earning himself the Iron Cross for his successful escapade a few weeks later.

Leicestershire's 'Thankful Villages'

'Thankful' or 'blessed' villages were so named because all of the men they sent off to the First World War returned home alive. Some fifty-three villages across England and Wales figure in their number. Leicestershire has three: Saxby, East Norton and Stretton en le Field.

No war memorials exist in these villages, but they do bear plaques in the church to celebrate those who fought and returned home alive.

The Carillion

By the end of the First World War, Loughborough had lost 400 men and a unique monument was built in the town: a campanile or bell tower was erected in Queens Park, containing forty-seven bells of differing sizes. The range of bells allowed a diverse range of musical notes, thus allowing bell ringers to play a large variety of tunes on a keyboard.

Donors had their names inscribed on the bells. One was Edmund Denis Taylor, the head of Taylor's bell foundry who forged the bells – and uncle of three of the lost.

The Second World War

Leicestershire Blitzes

Leicester survived the war with relatively few major bombings. But on 19 November 1940, the city was inundated with German bombs from 7.45 in the evening until the early hours of the following morning.

The worst of the bombing centred on the Highfields district of the city where forty people were killed. Buses were brought out in the blackout to evacuate residents, while others sought sanctuary on the open ground of Victoria Park. In those few hours over 150 high-explosive bombs were dropped on the city, killing 108 people, injuring 284, destroying 255 homes and 56 industrial premises.

The rest of the county suffered equally. In 1941, Kirby Muxloe was heavily bombed when a German bomber returning from a raid on Coventry emptied its load on two streets, destroying the Free Church and several houses. Gaps left in the houses can still be seen.

Earl Shilton was also targeted, suffering 192 air-raid alerts during the war, the first on 26 June 1940, the last on 20 March 1945. During one of those raids in November 1940, two parachute mines landed on the village. One mine failed to explode and there were no casualties.

The most frightening attack on the village occurred at 7 a.m. on 27 July 1942 when a lone German bomber attacked, dropping three stick bombs. Farm buildings were damaged and a bull so badly injured it had to be destroyed.

But it could have been much worse. Mr T.J. Langton, then an Earl Shilton schoolboy, recalls an event that occured to another boy, Gary Cassell:

> On this particular morning a lost German plane flew low over Keats Lane and … this plane flew over, low and sprayed machine gun bullets along Keats Lane. He ran into an entry and dropped his scarf. When he eventually recovered it, he noticed it contained

a bullet hole. He told the story to Michael Mortimore, the son of the village bobby who also attended the school. On hearing this, Mike Mortimore said it was a good job he had not got it wrapped round his neck at the time.

Barwell's Unexploded Bomb

Other bombs that fell didn't explode – well not immediately. Barwell was one such place where the army dealt with the device. The area around a 1-mile radius was cleared and locals were told to stay indoors while the experts did their work.

The army bomb disposal expert approached the bomb dressed for a speedy exit – in shorts and running shoes. But his careful detonation of the bomb had to be halted when learner fliers from the local Desford airbase took to the skies above, meaning a delay to the detonation.

Once the planes were clear it was back to work on the bomb. But disabling it was by no means smooth. Although no one was hurt, the nose of the bomb ended up in a greenhouse in nearby Elmesthorpe – a distance of just under 2 miles away!

Heroes and Heroines

Many Leicestershire folk have played their parts, big and small, in war and conflict. Here are just a few:

Richard Henry Burton (1923–1993) was awarded the Victoria Cross in the Second World War. Born in Melton Mowbray, Burton was a 21-year-old private when he took the lead in an attack near Florence, taking out enemy machine-gunners single-handedly so his platoon could move forward. He also continued to act with 'magnificent gallantry and total disregard of his own safety' later in the attack, despite many of his platoon being dead or wounded.

Elaine Sophie Plowman, *née* Browne Bartroli, was born in 1917 to a French mother and an English father. She lived in Leicester until the outbreak of the Second World War, when Elaine heard through her husband, an officer in the Royal Artillery, that special operations were looking for a young, French-speaking woman to go undercover to France as part of a sabotage operation.

Elaine volunteered and was recruited. In 1943, she was dropped into German-occupied France. There she assumed the identity of Madame Prunier, a Marseilles housewife, while surreptitiously carrying radio messages, as well as dynamite and fuses for sabotage.

On one occasion a German officer chanced to ask her for a light. Elaine had two boxes in her pocket: one of matches, the other containing a secret message she was delivering. She had no choice but to trust to blind luck and hand over one of the boxes – fortunately it was the one without the message.

Eventually her luck ran out when her cell was betrayed by a Gestapo agent who had infiltrated their circle. On 13 September 1944, Elaine Plowman was shot as a spy at Dachau concentration camp. After the war, she was posthumously awarded the Croix de Guerre and the King's Commendation for Bravery.

Other Heroes
Barrow is the birthplace of Air Vice Marshall Johnnie Johnson, who led many skirmishes in the Second World War and the Korean War.

Born in Leicester in 1900, Sydney (Syd) Lucas was the last solider to serve in both world wars. Syd joined up just three months before the end of the conflict in 1918 and was still in training when the war ended.

Ten years later, Syd and his wife emigrated to Australia and it was here he signed up again, this time with Australia's machine gun battalion. This time, Syd saw action. He was deployed to Palestine and assigned to guard Italian and German POWs before returning to Australia to work in an aircraft factory.

He died in 2008 at his home in Melbourne, Australia, at the age of 108.

But not all heroes were human. In 1914, a horse called Songster was drafted into the Leicestershire Yeomanry. He was assigned to trooper Bert Main of Loughborough and together they were sent to France at the start of the war.

Over 8 million horses and mules died in the conflict. But Songster came back. He became a local celebrity and was cared for by Sergeant Major Harry Poole on his farm in Woodhouse Eaves. Remarkably, he lived until 1940, when he died at the age of 40, to be buried on the farm that was his last home with his medal ribbons.

TERRORISM

Leicestershire has been the target of terrorists twice in the twentieth century. The first time was just before the outbreak of the Second World War. The IRA, taking advantage of the unsettled situation, were upping their attacks on the mainland. In June 1939, one of their operatives constructed and posted thirteen parcel bombs, designed to go off on a train to London.

The plan, if it had come off, would have caused a major disaster, but fortunately it never made it that far. Instead, five of the bombs went off accidentally in the Campbell Street sorting office. A postman received injuries to his hands and face but avoided serious harm. The rest of the bombs were quickly traced by the similar handwriting – and their fake London addresses – and disarmed by immersion in buckets of water.

The IRA struck again in 1990 – this time with a bomb attack on an army van parked on Rutland Street. But as in 1939, the attack was thwarted. The bomb fell off the back of the vehicle, exploding and shaking buildings within a 200-yard radius but claiming no fatalities. However, two army personnel and a civilian were treated for minor injuries.

ILLUSTRATION CREDITS

Andrews, William, *Bygone Leicestershire* (F. Murray, 1892)

Aubrey, William Hickman Smith, *The National and Domestic History of England ...With numerous steel plates, coloured pictures, etc.* (James Hagger: London, 1867)

Baldwin, Louisa, *The Shadow on the Blind and Other Ghost Stories* (J.M. Dent & Co.: London, 1895)

Brayley, E.W., *The graphic and historical illustrator; an original miscellany of literary, antiquarian, and topographical information embellished with one hundred and fifty woodcuts* (Chidley: London, 1834)

Cattermole, R., *The Great Civil War of Charles I and the Parliament* (Fisher, Son & Co.: London, 1846)

Cunningham, Henry S., *Lectures on the physiological laws of life, hygiene, and a general outline of diseases peculiar to females* (G.F. Borst & Co.: Indianapolis, 1882)

Elmhirst, Edward Pennell, *The cream of Leicestershire: eleven seasons' skimmings, notable runs and incidents of the chase, selected and republished from 'The Field'* (Routledge: London, 1883)

Hoffman, Professor, *Modern Magic: A Practical Treatise on the Art of Conjuring* (Routledge: London, 1885)

Hood, Thomas, *The Haunted House* (Lawrence and Bullen: London, 1896)

Ingoldsby, Thomas, *The Ingoldsby Legends* (E.P. Dutton & Co., 1907)

Jackson, William, *The New and Complete Newgate Calendar* (Gale Ecco, 2012)

Kendall, H.B., *The Origin and History of the Primitive Methodist Church* (Dalton: London, 1880)

Loudon, J.C., *An Encyclopedia of Agriculture* (Longman: London, 1831)

Loudon, J.C., *Trees and shrubs: an abridgment of the Arboretum et fruticetum britannicum: containing the hardy trees and schrubs of Britain, native* and foreign, scientifically and popularly described: with their propagation, culture and uses and engravings of nearly all the species. (F. Warne & Co.: London, 1875)

Loudon, J.C., *An encyclopædia of gardening; comprising the theory and practice of horticulture, floriculture, arboriculture, and landscape-gardening, including all the latest improvements; a general history of gardening in all countries; and a statistical view of its present state, with suggestions for its future progress, in the British Isles* (Longman: London, 1827)

Macaulay, T.B., *The Lays of Ancient Rome* (Longman: London, 1904)

Owen, Richard, *A History of British Fossil Reptiles Vol. II* (Cassell & Co., 1849)

Patriarchs, Militant Drill Regulations and Ceremonies (The Friedenwald Co.: Baltimore, 1898)

Savage, Charles C., *Illustrated biography; or, Memoirs of the great and the good of all nations and all times; comprising sketches of eminent statesmen, philosophers, heroes, artists, reformers, philanthropists, mechanics, navigators, authors, poets, divines, soldiers, savans, etc.* (Phinney & Co.: Buffalo, 1856)

Shirley, Evelyn Philip, *Some account of English deer parks, with notes on the management of deer* (J. Murray: London, 1867)

Traill, H.D., *Social England: a record of the progress of the people in religion, laws, learning, arts, industry, commerce, science, literature and manners, from the earliest times to the present day.* (Putnam: New York, 1901)

Unknown, *Library of the World's Best Literature, Ancient and modern* (University of California Libraries, 1896)

Winter, William, '*Gray Days and Gold ... New edition, revised, with illustrations*' (Macmillan & Co.: New York, 1896)

Youmans, E.L., *The Handbook of Household Science* (D. Appleton & Co.: New York, 1860)

BIBLIOGRAPHY

BOOKS AND DOCUMENTS

Bailey, Brian, *The Luddite Rebellion* (Sutton, 1998)

Billson, Charles James, *County Folklore of Leicestershire and Rutland* (Brownell Press, 2013)

Cantor, Leonard, *The Scheduled Ancient Monuments of Leicestershire and Rutland* (Kairos Press, 2003)

Carroll, Kevin K., *The Date of Boudicca's Revolt* (Britannia, vol. 10, 1979)

Clay, Patrick, *The Neolithic and Bronze Age of Leicestershire and Rutland* (Transactions of the Leicestershire archaeological and Historical Society, 73, 1999)

Copy of extract of information laid against Jane Clark of Wigston Magna and Joseph and Mary, her son and daughter in the case of witchcraft, held at the Leicester Assizes, August 1717

Crawford, Elizabeth, *The Suffragette Movement* (Routledge, 1999)

Crompton, James, *Leicestershire Lollards* (Leicestershire University Library)

Curtis, John, *Topographical History of the County of Leicester* (1831)

Hawkes, S.C., *A Late Roman Buckle from Tripontium* (Transactions of the Birmingham and Warwickshire Archaeological Society, 1972, Vol. 85 pp. 144–159)

Henry of Knighton, *Knighton's Chronicle 1337–1396* (edited and translated by G.H. Martin, Clarendon Press: Oxford)

Hoskins, W.G., *The Anglian and Scandinavian Settlement of Leicestershire* (Anon., 1935)

Leicestershire Guild of Storytellers, *Leicestershire and Rutland Folk Tales* (The History Press, 2013)

Millward, Roy, *A History of Leicestershire and Rutland* (Phillimore, 1985)

Newitt, Ned, *The Slums of Leicester* (JMD Media Ltd, 2013)

Owen, C. *The Leicestershire and South Derbyshire Coalfield 1200–1900* (Ashbourne: Moorland, 1984)

Palmer, Roy, *The Folklore of Leicestershire and Rutland* (Sycamore Press, 1985)

Patterson, Temple A., *Radical Leicester* (Leicester University Press, 1954)

Pen Lloyd, Col., *The History of the Mysterious Papillon Hall* (Leicestershire Local History Council)

Powell, T.G.E., *Late Bronze Age Hoard From Welby* (*The Archaeological Journal*, Vol. 105, Issue 1, 1948)

Randall, J.L., A *History of the Meynell Hounds and Country, 1780–1901* (Nabu Press, 2010)

Sheldon, Natasha, *Leicester in 100 Dates* (The History Press, 2014)
——, *Not a Guide to Leicester* (The History Press, 2013)

Skinner, Julia, *Leicestershire and Rutland a Miscellany* (Francis Frith Collection, 2012)
——, *Leicestershire and Rutland Recipes* (Francis Frith Collection, 2012)

Smith, Julia, *Leicester and Rutland Miscellany* (Identity Books, 2012)

Specification of Thomas Crick AD *1853, No. 542* (County Record Office)

Squires, Anthony and Jeeves, Michael, *Leicestershire and Rutland Woodlands Past and Present* (Kairos Press, 1994)

Stevenson, Joan and Squires, Anthony, *Bradgate Park: The Childhood Home of Lady Jane Grey* (Kairos Press, 1999)

Stones, E., *The Folvilles of Ashby Folville, Leicestershire, and Their Associates in Crime, 1326–1347* (Transactions of the Royal historical Society 77, 1956)

Thompson, James, *The History of Leicester: From the Time of the Romans to the End of the Seventeenth Century* (J.S.C. Rossley, 1849)
——, *The History of the Borough of Leicester in the Eighteenth Century* (Crossley and Clarke, 1871)

Tomlin, R.S.O., *Non Coritani Sed Corieltauvi* (The Antiquaries Journal) 1983, Vol. LXIII, Part II, pp.353–62)

Westwood, Jennifer, *Albion: A Legendary Guide to Britain* (Granada Publishing Ltd, 1985)

Wright, Andrew James, *Ghosts and Hauntings In and Around Leicestershire* (Heart of Albion Press, 2006)
——, *Haunted Leicestershire* (Tempus Publishing, 2005)

NEWSPAPERS AND JOURNALS

Gentleman's Magazine, 1813

Leicester and Nottingham Journal

Leicester Daily Post

Leicester Evening Mail

Leicester Guardian

Leicester Illustrated Chronicle, 1856–1979

Leicester Journal

Leicester Mail

Leicester Mercury, 1874

Leicester Pioneer

Melton Times

Telegraph

WEBSITES

BBC: www.news.bbc.co.uk

British History Online: www.british-history.ac.uk

British Museum: www.britishmuseum.org/research/research_projects/
all_current_projects/the_east_leicestershire_hoards.aspx

Capital Punishment UK: www.capitalpunishmentuk.org

Centre on Dynamics of Ethnicity: www.ethnicity.ac.uk/medialibrary/
briefings/localdynamicsofdiversity/ethnic-and-religious-mixing-in-
leicestershire.pdf

Charnwood Council: www.charnwood.gov.uk/listed_buildings/
hill_fort_enclosure_and_linear_boundary_beacon_hill_woodhouse

Encyclopedia Britannica: www.britannica.com

Fossils UK: ukfossils.co.uk/2003/11/07/ketton-quarry/

Heraldry of the World: www.ngw.nl/heraldrywiki/index.
php?title=Leicestershire

Historic England: https://historicengland.org.uk/listing/the-list/list-
entry/1008549

Historic UK: www.historic-uk.com/CultureUK/Fox-Hunting-in-
Britain/

Leicester City Council: www.Leicester.gov.uk

Leicester City Football Club: www.lcfc.com/club/history/leicester_
fosse.aspx

Leicestershire County Council: www.leics.gov.uk

Leicestershire County Cricket Club: www.leicestershireccc.co.uk/lccc-history.html

Leicestershire County Parks: www.leicscountryparks.org.uk/jubilee-woods/

Leicestershire Police: www.leics.police.uk/about-us/our-history/180-years

The Leicestershire and South Derbyshire Coal Field: http://www.nmrs.org.uk/mines-map/coal-mining-in-the-british-isles/leicestershire/

Leicestershire Statistics and Research: www.lsr-online.org/leicestershire.html

Leicestershire Villages Oral Histories: www.le.ac.uk/emoha/community/leicsvillages.html

Martin, R.E., 'The Legends, Folklore and Dialect of Leicestershire with an Introduction on the General History of the County' (www.le.ac.uk/lahs/downloads)

National Forest: www.nationalforest.org/forest/

NERC Open Research Archive: http://nora.nerc.ac.uk/8675/

Ordnance Survey: www.ordnancesurvey.co.uk/blog/2014/08/where-is-the-centre-of-great-britain-2/

Outlaws and Highwaymen: www.outlawsandhighwaymen.com

Paranormal Database: www.paranormaldatabase.com/leicestershire/leicdata.php

Parliament UK: www.parliament.uk/about/living-

Prison Voices: www.prisonvoices.org/?p=3522

Real Crime: www.real-crime.co.uk

Rugby Archaeological Society: www.rugbyarchaeology.org.uk/index.php/tripontium

Shepshed: www.shepshed.org/History.htm

Stilton Cheese: www.stiltoncheese.co.uk/history_of_stilton

Swannington Heritage: www.swannington-heritage.co.uk/swannington_village_history.html

The University of Leicester: www.le.ac.uk

The Wildlife Trust: www.lrwt.org.uk/wildlife/wildlife-leicestershire-rutland/

The Woodland Trust: www.woodlandtrust.org.uk/